MW01617941

Trenton

THE GOLDEN TWENTIES

Portraits & Figure Paintings by Joseph Kleitsch

PASADENA MUSEUM *of* CALIFORNIA ART

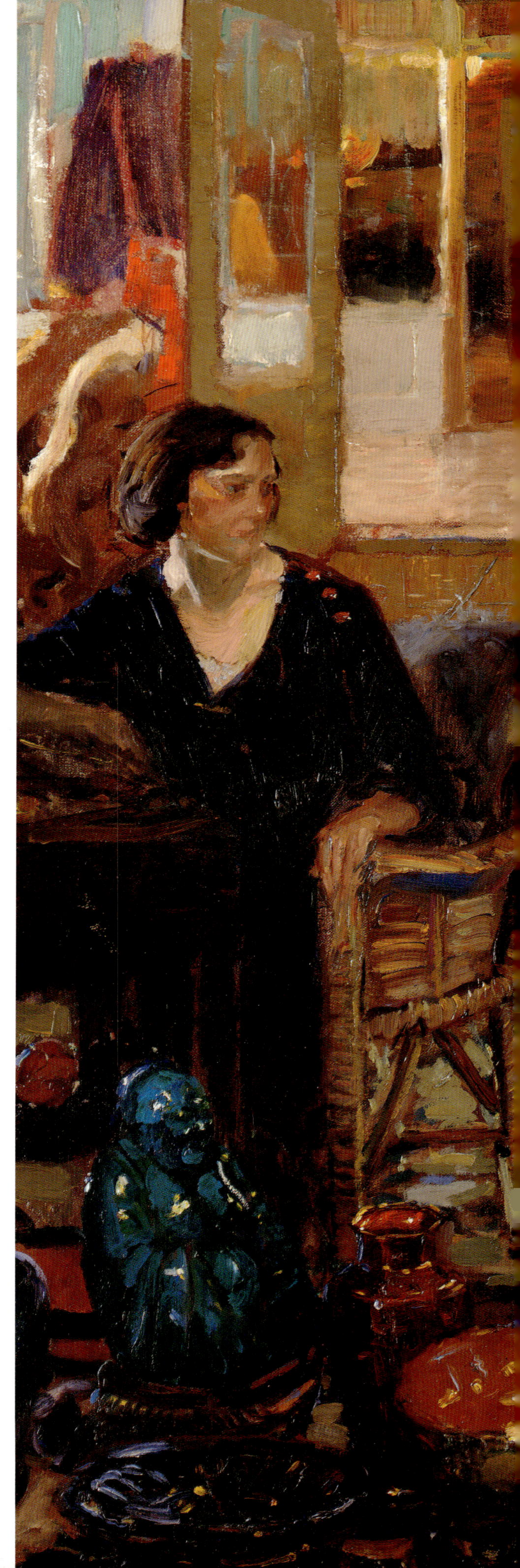

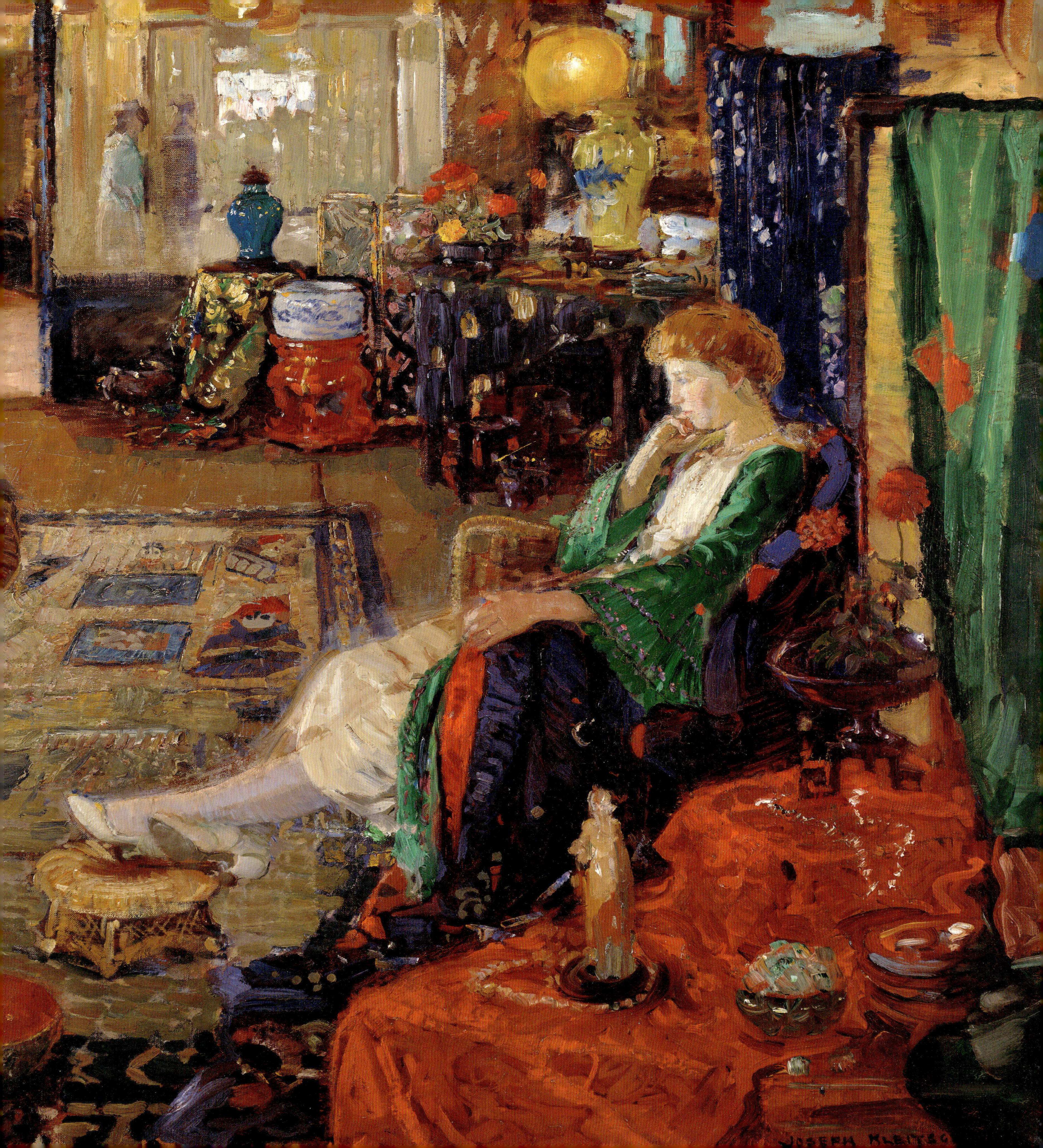

This catalogue was published on the occasion of the exhibition *The Golden Twenties: Portraits and Figure Paintings by Joseph Kleitsch,* curated by Dr. Patricia Trenton and organized by the Pasadena Museum of California Art, March 5–August 6, 2017.

Published by the
Pasadena Museum of California Art
490 East Union Street
Pasadena, CA 91101
(626) 568-3665
http://pmcaonline.org

ISBN: 978-0-9770408-1-0
PCN: 2016947219

Editor: Jean Patterson
Designer: Lilli Colton
Printed in China

Reproduction credits:
Photos © Gerard Vuilleumier: cover, pp. 6, 10, 12, 22, 28, 38, 42–43, 44, 47, 48, 51, 53, 55, 59, 61, 69, 71, 73, 75, 77, 79, 81, 89, 91, 95, 97, 103, 104, 107, 113, 115, 117, 123, 125, 127, 128, 131, 140
Photos © Christopher Bliss: pp. 32, 85, 111, 119, 135
Photos © Jesse Bravo: frontispiece, pp. 41, 65, 87, 133
Photo © Asa Gilmore: p. 99
Photos courtesy of Bonhams: pp. 16, 19, 27, 35

Cover, front: *Miss Ketchum* (detail), c. 1918. Oil on canvas, 42 x 36 inches. Private Collection

Cover, back: *Portrait of Isador Berger (Rhapsody)* (detail), 1917. Oil on canvas, 40 x 30 inches. Private Collection

Frontispiece: *The Oriental Shop* (detail), 1922. Oil on canvas, 32 x 40 inches. Crocker Art Museum, Melza and Ted Barr Collection

CONTENTS

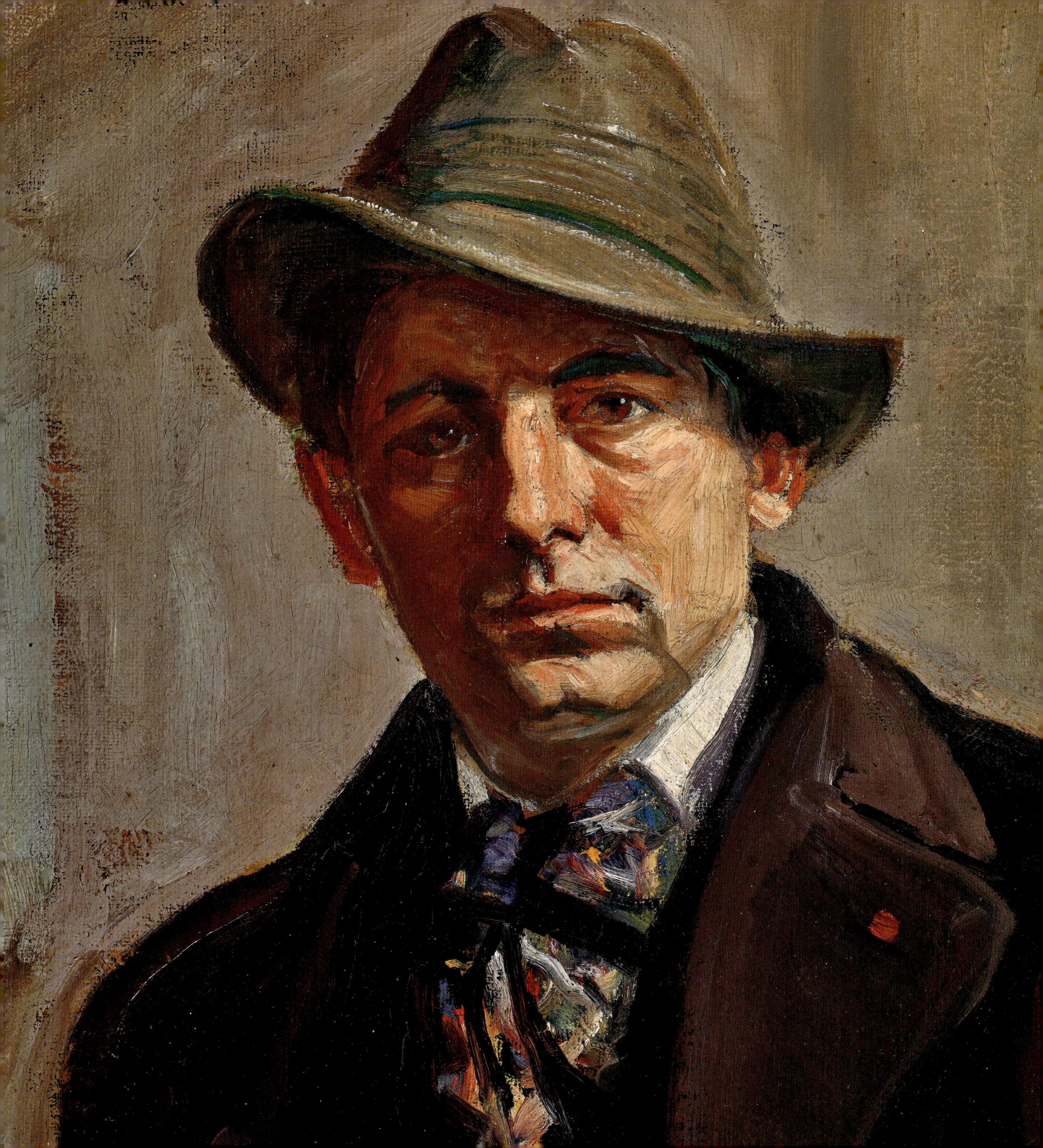

FOREWORD

A NATIVE OF HUNGARY, painter Joseph Kleitsch (1882–1931) did not arrive in the Golden State until 1920, by way of Chicago. Although his life was tragically cut short by a heart attack in 1931, during those eleven years in California he produced his most masterful works. His career is often divided into two distinct periods, the first as a portraitist in Chicago and the second as a painter of impressionistic landscapes in California. However, this is an inaccurate oversimplification of his oeuvre. Kleitsch remained dedicated to producing portraits and figurative scenes throughout his career. These works evolved over time, becoming increasingly impressionistic in palette and brushstroke, and then more compositionally complex and abstract in response to his travels and studies. His scenes are imbued with the color and decorative patterns of his native Hungary as well as the light and style of both Chicago and, then, California. But it is the sensitivity of Kleitsch's approach to his figurative work that reveals why he became known as the premier portraitist of Laguna Beach shortly after moving to that artists' haven. Each portrait and figurative work acquaints the viewer with intimate aspects of his subjects and locales, revealing the distinctive personalities, demeanors, and essences of Laguna Beach during the Golden Twenties.

Self-Portrait (detail), 1915
Oil on canvas, 40 x 30 inches
Collection of James Taylor and Gary Conway

The focused nature of *The Golden Twenties: Portraits and Figure Paintings by Joseph Kleitsch* continues the Pasadena Museum of California Art's mission to present the breadth of California art and design through exhibitions that explore the cultural dynamics and influences that are unique to California. Like other PMCA projects, the specificity of this exhibition reveals a vital aspect of California art in need of further exploration and facilitates a more complete understanding of the art and culture of the state.

The Golden Twenties builds on decades of research by Dr. Patricia Trenton and the book she wrote for The Irvine Museum, *Joseph Kleitsch: A Kaleidoscope of*

Color. I have to begin by thanking Joan Irvine Smith and James Irvine Swinden of The Irvine Museum for leading the charge with this significant contribution to California art.

Dr. Patricia Trenton is one of the preeminent scholars of California art and a thorough researcher with a zeal for scholarship and a great attention to detail. Her seminal contributions to California art history date back to 1987 and the exhibition and publication *California Light, 1900–1930* and continued with her pioneering project *Independent Spirits: Women Painters of the American West, 1890–1945*.

The PMCA has benefitted from Dr. Trenton's scrupulous research during her past collaborations with the Museum, including *The Not-So-Still Life* in 2003, and *Edgar Payne: The Scenic Journey* in 2012. We are thrilled to have her as our curator for *The Golden Twenties: Portraits and Figure Paintings by Joseph Kleitsch*. The success of the project is largely due to her insight.

I am indebted to the supporters of *The Golden Twenties* exhibition and catalogue who gave through the California Visionary Fund. First and foremost, we are grateful to Lead Patrons Earlene and Herbert Seymour. We also thank Presenting Patrons Christine and Reed Halladay; Underwriting Patrons Simon K. Chiu, Lori and Jeff Hyland, and Bob and Arlene Oltman; Benefactor Patrons Yvonne Boseker, and Gail and Peter Ochs; Sustaining Patrons Bram and Sandra Dijkstra, Michael Feddersen, Penny and Jay Lusche, Gayle and Ed Roski, and Irene and George Stern; and Contributing Patrons Susan and Robert Ehrlich, Jerrold and Judith Felsenthal, Joyce and Tom Leddy, Tobey Moss and Allen Moss, Mel and Betty Sembler, Carol and Cliff Trenton, and Ruth Westphal; and Supporting Patrons Robert and Nadine Hall, and Allen and Dottie Lay. I also acknowledge the contributions of the following Visionaries: Gina Knox, Susan and Jim Crawford, Brooke Abercrombie and Christopher Wilson, Jeff Dutra, Diane and Van Simmons, William C. Georges, Reba White Williams, Hannah and Russel Kully, Kathleen Lombard Smyk, Betsey Tyler, Janet G. Michaels, Lauren Frankel, Diane Asselin Baer, Ann and Dan Selmi, Randy and Mary Short, Jonas B. Siegel, and Lawrence H. Title.

Additionally, my utmost thanks to the Historical Collections of California Art and its members for providing a significant grant to support this important project.

I also thank John Moran Auctioneers, Bonhams Auctioneers, and The Redfern Gallery for their generous support.

We are also appreciative of the lenders who have parted with important works for the duration of the exhibition. Special thanks to many anonymous lenders, and to Simon K. Chiu, Stephen P. Diamond, Robert and Susan Ehrlich, Michael Feddersen, Reed and Christine Halladay, W. Donald Head, James W. and Sarah T. Miller, Linda and David O'Hoy, Mary Olden, Larane Rodnick, Herbert and Earlene Seymour, Barbara and Thomas B. Stiles II, James Taylor and Gary Conway, as well as the Barlow Respiratory Hospital, Crocker Art Museum, George Stern Fine Arts, The Irvine Museum, The Kelley Gallery, Laguna Art Museum, Michael Kizhner Fine Art, Orange County Museum of Art, and The Redfern Gallery.

We are grateful to the PMCA Ambassador and previous PMCA board member Simon K. Chiu for his unwavering support of the Museum and his assistance with the exhibition and catalogue. Once again, I have to thank Gerard Vuilleumier for photographing the artworks and for his involvement with the catalogue. Special thanks are also owed to Josh Hardy, Ray Redfern, and George Stern for their assistance. I also thank Lilli Colton for designing this beautiful catalogue and Jean Patterson for her editing.

I have the deepest gratitude for the PMCA Board of Directors and Ambassador Circle Members for their support. I thank the PMCA Director of Exhibitions Erin Aitali for overseeing the project and Lead Preparator and Special Projects Manager Emmett Clements for tirelessly preparing the exhibition layout. I am ever appreciative of the significant contributions of Sergio Gomez, Alexis Kaneshiro, Sarah Mitchell, Brianna Smyk, and Susan Wang.

Lastly, we thank Dr. Patricia Trenton for her unyielding devotion to California art. One of the most respected scholars in the field, Dr. Trenton has devoted over fifty years to furthering the art of this state. The PMCA is honored to work with her and to present the result of our collaboration, this exhibition and catalogue, to our audience.

Jenkins Shannon
Executive Director, 2009–16

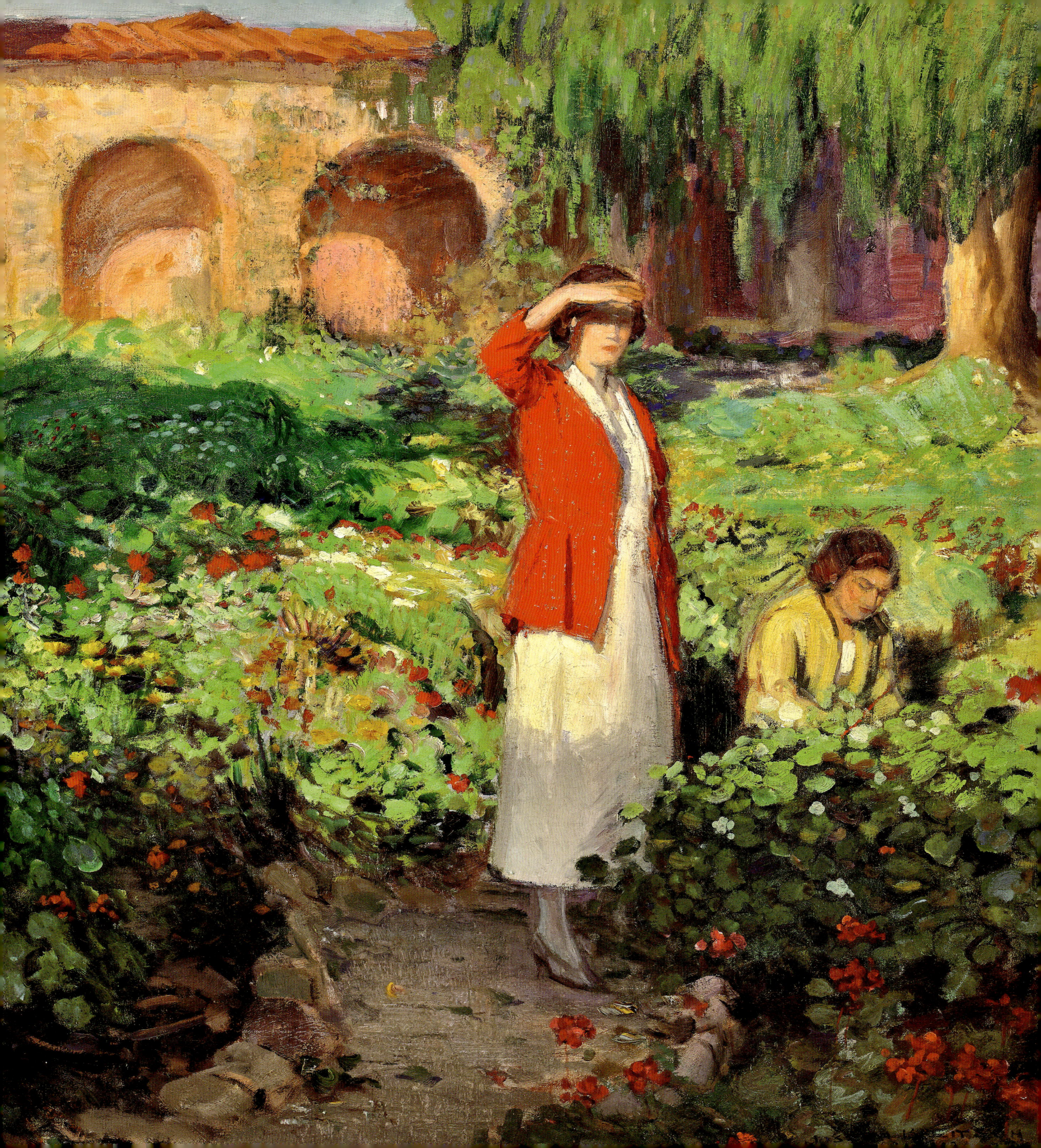

PREFACE

THE IRVINE MUSEUM was founded in 1992. Our mission is to preserve, document, and display the art of California dating from 1880 to 1940. The museum has published a number of books on this subject, and specifically on several of the important artists of the period. From the first, we identified Joseph Kleitsch as one of the important figures of California Impressionism, and in keeping with our mission statement, The Irvine Museum published *Joseph Kleitsch: A Kaleidoscope of Color*, by Dr. Patricia Trenton, in 2007. The book is remarkable not only for its comprehensive account of the life of the artist, but also for its thorough documentation of the artist's work, containing over three hundred plates of paintings and archival photographs.

I am delighted that The Irvine Museum is once again collaborating with the Pasadena Museum of California Art. Our museum has enjoyed a warm and productive relationship with PMCA and with Jenkins Shannon, its Executive Director from 2009 to 2016. Our two institutions collaborated most notably on the 2010–11 Franz A. Bischoff retrospective and accompanying catalogue, written by Mr. Jean Stern, Executive Director of The Irvine Museum, and Dr. Scott Shields, Associate Director and Chief Curator of the Crocker Art Museum in Sacramento.

I am further pleased to know that Dr. Patricia Trenton, the author of our book, is the Guest Curator of the Joseph Kleitsch exhibition at PMCA. Dr. Trenton is widely recognized as the leading authority on Kleitsch's life and work. I am confident that this exhibition will be an important contribution to the history of California art and that the works selected for display will meet the highest standards of American art.

James Irvine Swinden
President, The Irvine Museum

Red and Green (Mission San Juan Capistrano) (detail), 1923
Oil on canvas, 36 x 40 inches
The Irvine Museum

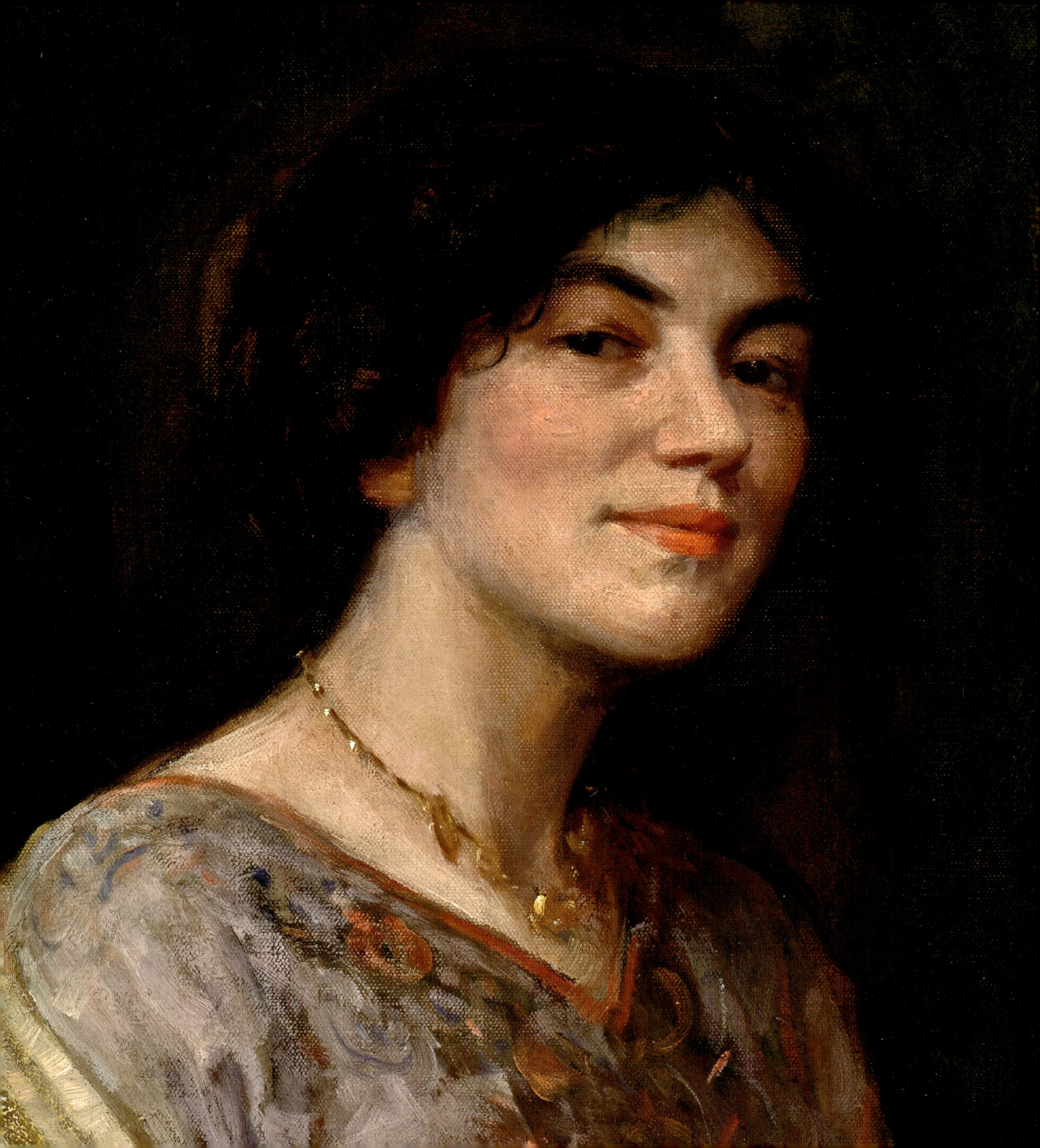

ACKNOWLEDGMENTS

SOME THIRTY-THREE YEARS AGO I was fortunately introduced to the historic plein-air paintings of Southern California. Among the many talented artists of the region, Joseph Kleitsch immediately captured my eye with his vigorous brushwork, brash use of paint, and vibrant colors. He was an obvious talent—unpredictable, but so interesting in the manner of how he chose his subjects. His reputation as an exceptional artist had escalated him to the highest of professional ranks. During his lifetime, he was praised by art critics and his peers, only to fall into the cracks of obscurity after his premature death, in 1931.

The first publication to resurrect his career was my exhibition catalogue titled *California Light, 1900–1930,* published by Laguna Art Museum in 1990. Seventeen years later, in 2007, The Irvine Museum and its President, James Swinden, published *Joseph Kleitsch: A Kaleidoscope of Color,* a comprehensive account of Kleitsch's biography and distinguished art career, showcasing the virtuosity of his artwork and talent. For me it was an opportune time to praise and honor my favorite plein-air artist. The Pasadena Museum of California Art's 2017 exhibition, accompanied by this catalogue, focuses on Kleitsch's portraits and figurative paintings and provides a platform for discussions of the artist's work in this genre.

The lack of a personal archive or exhibition record for Kleitsch resulted for me in fifteen years of devoted research on the artist's life and career. To carry out this mission, I turned to a large number of people who volunteered their time to assist me in the realization of this project. In particular, I express my gratitude and fond friendship to researchers Janet Murphy and Eric Jessen for their expert assistance and the time that they devoted to this mission, which cannot be measured.

To Janet Blake, Curator of Historical Art at Laguna Art Museum, I express my appreciation for her willingness to share with me the museum's large archive of materials and photographs related to California plein-air painters.

Miss Gregg (detail), c. 1919
Oil on canvas, 48 x 30 inches
Collection of Michael Kizhner Fine Art

I would be remiss if I did not acknowledge the many dealers and collectors who provided photographs of Kleitsch paintings: George Stern of George Stern Fine Arts; Ray Redfern of The Redfern Gallery; DeWitt McCall of DeRu's Fine Arts; the late Al Stendahl, Ron and April Dammann of Stendahl Galleries; Scot Levitt, Vice President and Director of Fine Arts at Bonhams; and James Carona of Heather James Fine Art. Two other dealers, David O'Hoy and Michael Kelley, who spent considerable time on Kleitsch research and are passionately devoted to the artist, have my deepest gratitude for their many contributions to this study.

During my fifteen years of research, many individuals generously supported the Kleitsch project throughout the United States and in Europe. It would be impossible to name them all here, but many have been mentioned in my other two Kleitsch publications. A special expression of gratitude is extended to them for their invaluable assistance.

Model's Throne (detail), c. 1928
Oil on canvas, 40 x 30 inches
Collection of Paul and
Kathleen Bagley

As for the collectors who have so generously loaned their paintings, I am certainly indebted to them for their willingness to share with the Pasadena Museum of California Art their wonderful Kleitsch portraits and figurative paintings to make this an exciting presentation. I would be remiss in not mentioning Ambassador Circle member and friend Simon K. Chiu, who directed many hours to the photography of the paintings with talented photographer Gerard Vuilleumier. Simon's advice and counsel have been invaluable.

To the museum staff, I express my gratitude for their time, patience, and assistance in making this a successful exhibition. In particular, Erin Aitali, Director of Exhibitions & Interim Associate Director, took on the large project of providing loan material to the collectors. At the helm, there is always a director who steers the ship and propels everything forward to a rewarding conclusion. Thank you, Jenkins Shannon, Executive Director of the Pasadena Museum of California Art, 2009–16, for your support and belief in my abilities to make a lasting contribution to the museum. I also owe editor Jean Patterson and designer Lilli Colton a debt of gratitude for their superb assistance.

Not lastly, but an important part of my life, how do I go about expressing my love and gratitude to my spouse, Norman (NB), for his contributions to the Kleitsch project? His understanding, support, patience, and continual reviewing of my written material took hours of his time. I express my deepest love and gratitude for his generous and kind ways.

Patricia Trenton

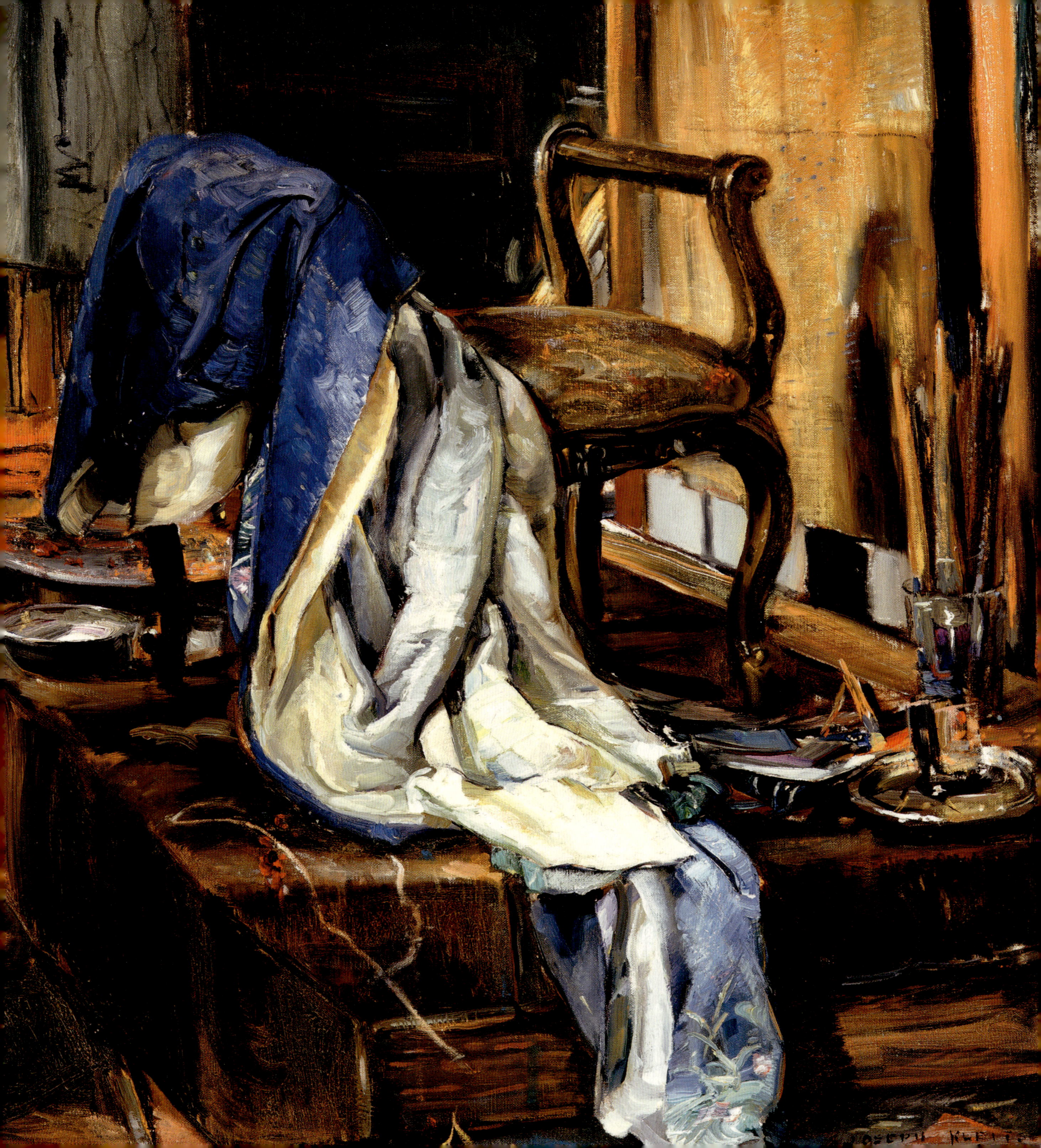

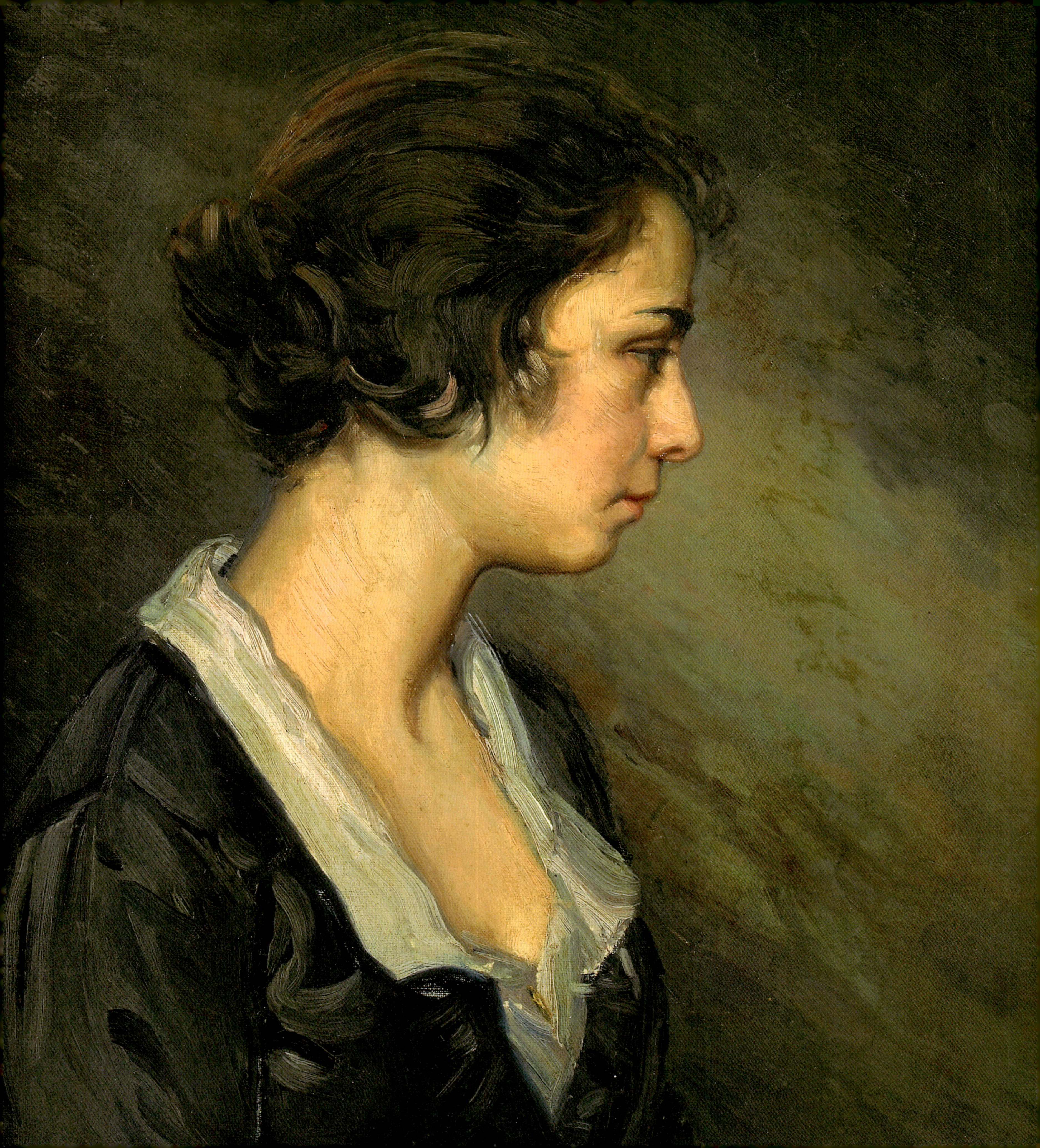

THE GOLDEN TWENTIES

JOSEPH KLEITSCH (1882–1931) IMMIGRATED to the United States from Hungary shortly after the turn of the twentieth century. After establishing himself as a highly sought-after portrait painter in Chicago, he moved to California in 1920 and became strongly identified with that state, particularly the town of Laguna Beach. His career fully blossomed during the Golden Twenties. From this period of time until his death in 1931, the country's parade of history brought about many changes to the lifestyles of Americans: the horror of the First World War, the Ku Klux Klan (promotion of white supremacy), the ratification of women's suffrage, the Roaring Twenties, or the Jazz Age, commercial enterprise and prosperity, and eventually the Golden Twenties, a prosperous period of consumerism and innovation that was cut short by the devastating Depression years. These tumultuous changes in a relatively short period of time in American history affected Kleitsch as well as other Americans.

Sicilian Girl (detail), c. 1919
Oil on canvas, 24 x 18 inches
Collection of Robert D. Lindner, Jr.

In addition to painting commissioned portraits, Kleitsch was a prolific landscape and figurative painter. He was unique among his fellow California artists in terms of the diversity of his subjects, his openness to various forms of creative expression, his intensity, and his eagerness to preserve a visual record of the remarkable historic sites of his adopted state.

In 1931, just before Kleitsch's sudden death, Southern California art critic Sonia Wolfson offered insight into his ever-changing moods and artistic approaches: "[He] is the most perverse person I ever met. Artistically and personally. He's the despair of the art dealer, the bane of the reviewer. He can't be labeled, classified, pigeon-holed or otherwise definitely and securely rubber-stamped, which is to his credit, but a source of pathetic bewilderment to his followers." Wolfson continued, "Kleitsch's artistic appetite . . . happen[s] to be remarkably discriminating, active, vastly and diversely absorbing! . . . Because of his perversity, which spells diversity, he gives infinite joy" (*Topics of the Town*, April 19, 1931).

California and Chicago art critics of the day acknowledged that Kleitsch was an exceptional portraitist above and beyond his peers. In 1919, Chicago critic William Pattison wrote a laudatory article comparing Kleitsch's masterful portraits "to those of such notable artists as the Spaniard Joaquin Sorolla y Bastida (1863–1923) as well as Rembrandt and other painters of the Dutch School" (*Fine Arts Journal*, June 1919). Southern California critic Antony Anderson later described the artist as a "brilliant portrait painter of beautiful women" (*South Coast News*, May 3, 1929).

As mentioned above, Kleitsch found his first sustained success as a portrait painter in Chicago, where he lived from 1913 to 1920. There, he established a studio and laid the foundation for a successful career in portraiture. His membership in the Palette and Chisel Club and in other local artists' associations forged his public persona and reputation. The artist used the Palette and Chisel Club as a springboard into Chicago's art and social mainstreams. Though he had had only rudimentary art training from a local itinerant in his native town of Német Szent Mihály, he soon developed the ability to paint identifiable portraits in a realistic mode.

Highlights (detail), c. 1928
Oil on canvas, 38 x 46 inches
Private Collection

Kleitsch was incurably restless, exploring the possibilities of his artistry by throwing himself into events, exhibitions, and activities related to his associations. He undertook a brief formal study at the Saturday School of the Art Institute of Chicago, where he drew and painted live models. When he painted at his studio in the Athenaeum Building, his primary models were his relatives and friends, as well as club members and their families. He submitted works to the annuals of the Art Institute of Chicago and the Palette and Chisel Club, and he entered into the spirit of the club's several "fantastical" parties each year. He lent his talent as a musician to the club's "Vodvil" show as the conductor of a small band of musician members. Apparently, Kleitsch also played the violin, flute, and accordion, as shown in the profusion of objects depicted in a 1928 autobiographical still life titled *Highlights*. The artistic discussions held at the Palette and Chisel Club made him aware of modern art and freed him to transition away from nineteenth-century forms and techniques. This awareness of progressive art would become most evident in his Laguna Beach street scenes, painted in the late 1920s after his return from a European trip and further exposure to art trends. Kleitsch and most of his fellow California artists still remained a world apart from radical changes and innovations in art, such as Fauvism, Cubism, Dadaism, and Expressionism.

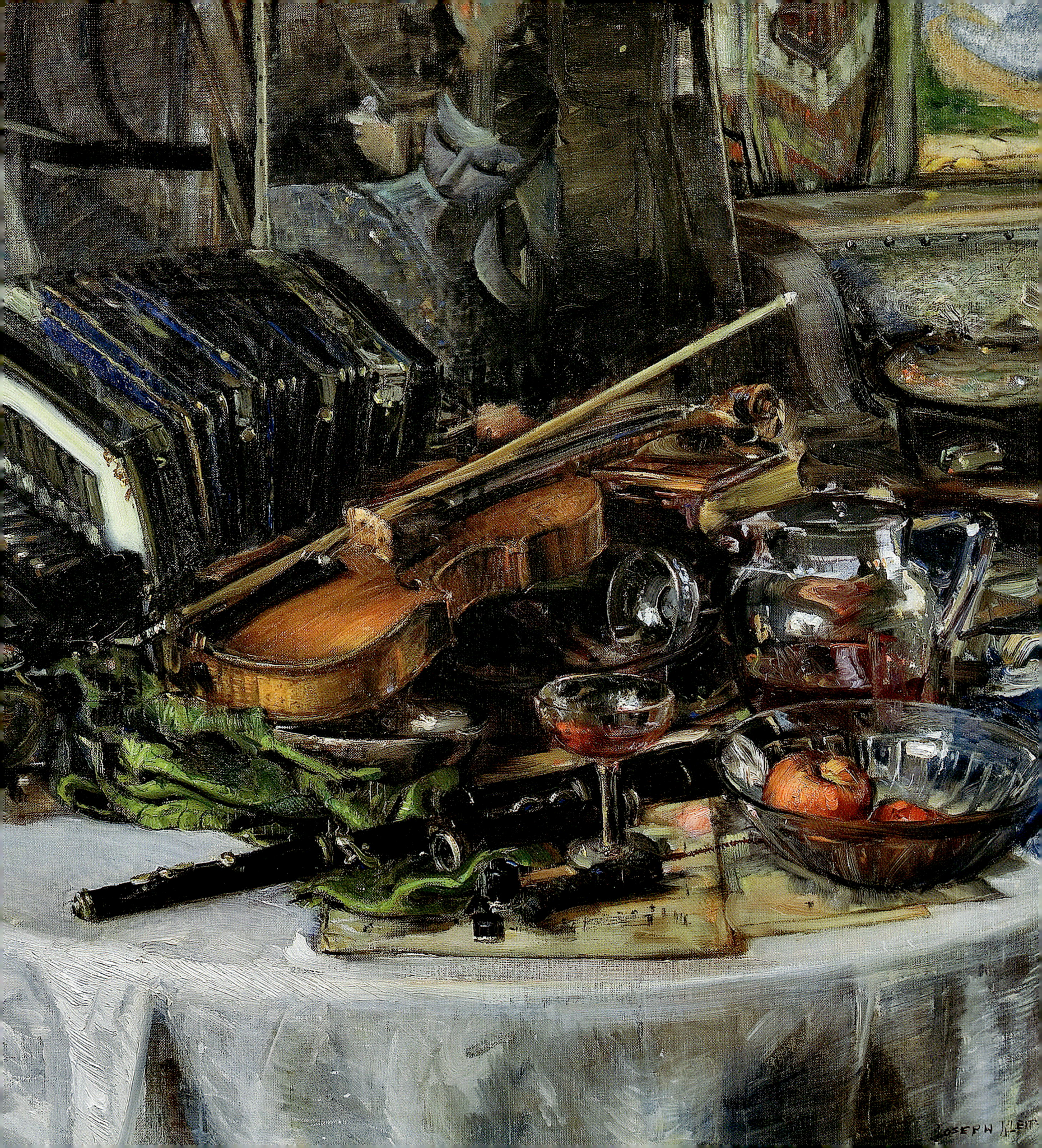
JOSEPH KLEIT

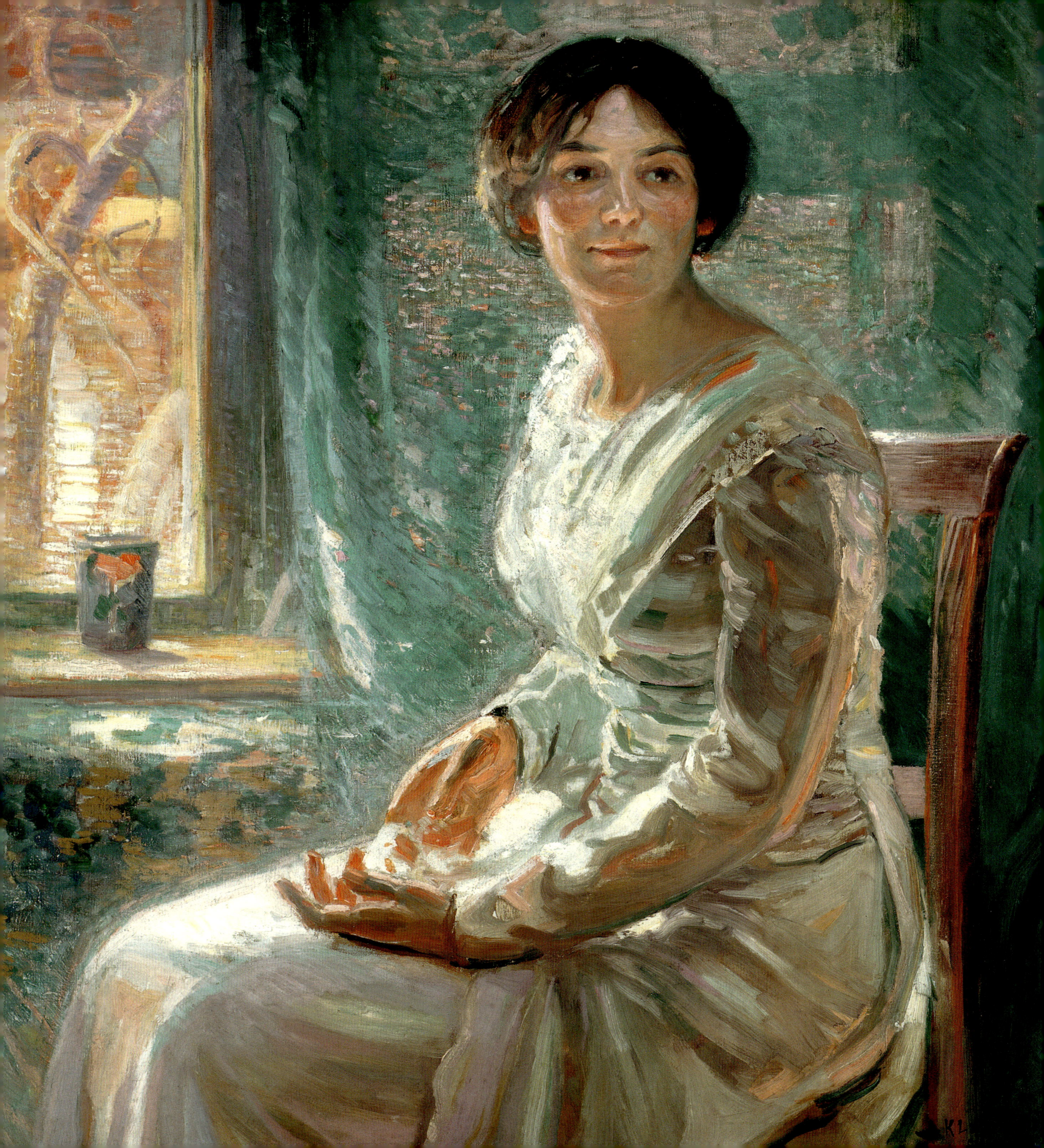

The popularity of portraiture in Chicago and the opportunities for compensation undoubtedly influenced the artist's decision to concentrate on this genre. In addition to painting portraits of friends and relatives, he painted half- and full-length portraits of himself and his young wife Edna in various attitudes and dress. In a striking portrait of Edna titled *Portrait of Mrs. K* (1916), he began to experiment with an impressionistic technique, a blond palette, and placement of the figure near a well-illuminated window. In a rare watercolor self-portrait, painted after America entered World War I in 1917, he portrays himself as a mature Chicago citizen whose reaction to America's intervention in the war is evidenced by his sober demeanor.

One of the high points of Kleitsch's tenure in Chicago was the acceptance of his *Self-Portrait* of 1919 (p. 133) for the Art Institute's Thirty-Second Annual Exhibition of American Oil Paintings and Sculpture, held that same year. This was an indication that East Coast artists no longer enjoyed exclusivity in this exhibition. Kleitsch's acceptance in the open competition was a boon for his career and gained him a secure place in his chosen genre. This particular self-portrait shows the serious and professional side of the artist, who was driven to advance his career, and it marks a significant transition in his life.

Portrait of Mrs. K (detail), 1916
Oil on canvas, 45 x 35 inches
Collection of Jim and Kathy Busby

Kleitsch's sudden move to California in 1920 came as a surprise to many, since his career as a portraitist was well established in Chicago. The author believes that the artist fully recognized the opportunities offered by the rapid expansion of cities in Southern California. The area's dynamic growth, temperate climate, and unique quality of light held an attraction for many artists. Its mild weather gave Kleitsch the opportunity to pursue his new interest in landscape painting, as he continued to be recognized for his special talent and achievement as a portrait painter. Some of his fellow Chicago artists had already established studios in Southern California; the prominent artist Edgar Payne, for instance, had settled in Laguna Beach and founded the Laguna Beach Art Association in 1918. Kleitsch was later invited to become an active member of this well-established artists' group.

Kleitsch and his family established residence in a small cottage in Laguna. This stimulating environment had an immediate and positive effect on his art, and it was certainly a healthier place for his wife and son, an improvement on the severe Chicago winters.

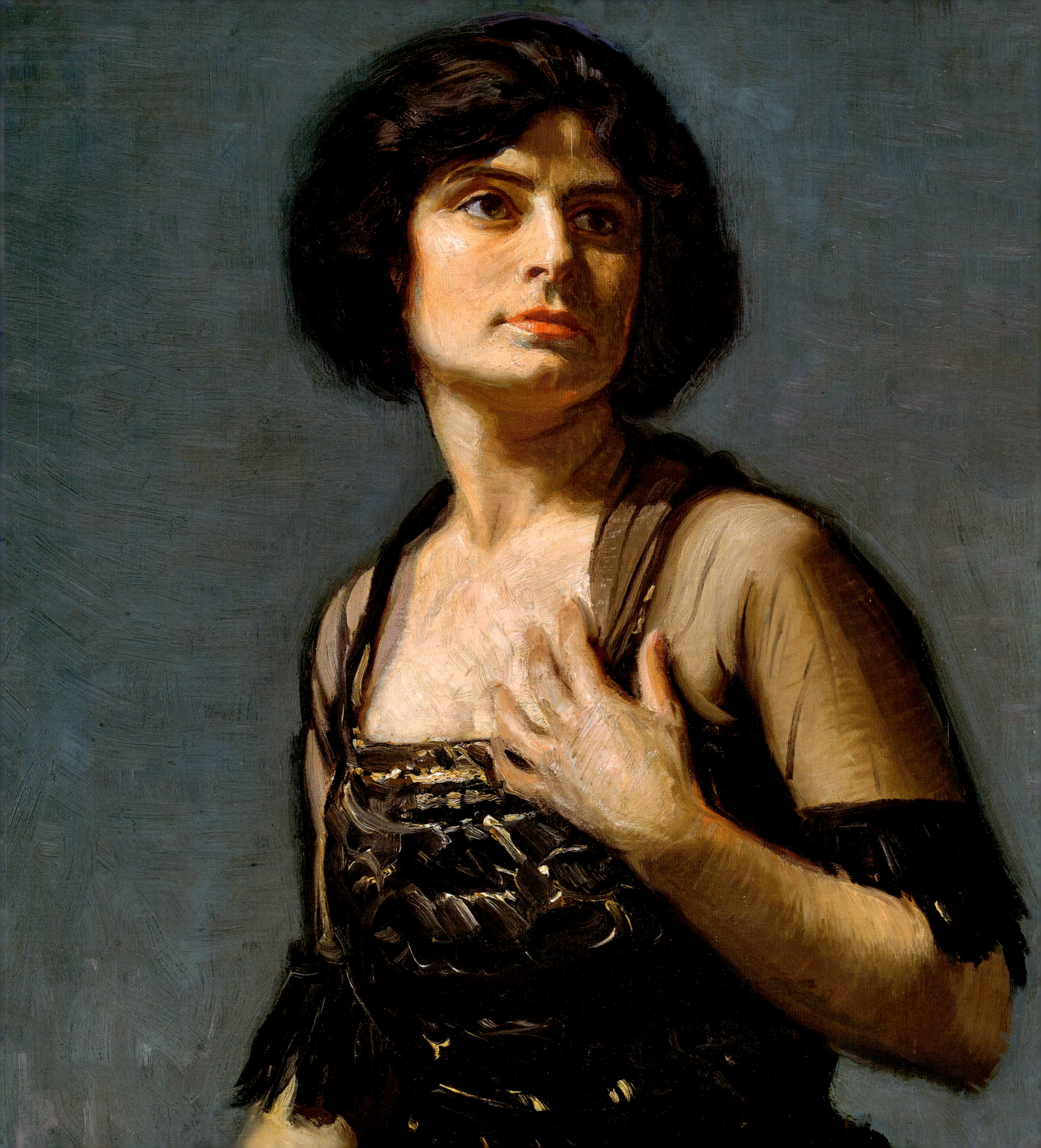

During the first half of the 1920s, Kleitsch painted portraits of patrons in Pasadena, Laguna, and Santa Ana. The distinguished Russian silent-film actress Hedda Nova sat for her portrait during her brief residency in Laguna, and it was exhibited at the Laguna Beach Art Association Gallery in May 1920. It was there that Kleitsch received many favorable comments from art critics, which led to the recognition of his talents by other artists. In his half-length portrait of Nova, the sitter is depicted wearing a seductive black, bouffant evening gown, with her full, bobbed hair styled in keeping with the sultry look of the 1920s. By year's end, Kleitsch was considered the dominant portraitist in the Southern California community, and he continued to attract commissions from many prominent citizens.

The film industry provided various patrons for portraits, primarily through the contacts of the prominent Los Angeles dealer Earl Stendahl, who contracted Kleitsch in 1922 to be an in-house portraitist, specifically to handle commissions. From 1921 to 1931, the Stendahl Galleries were located at the Ambassador—a new, elegant hotel with many shops and a diversity of dining choices that attracted the celebrities of the day. Under the dealer's aegis, Kleitsch's art was regularly exhibited in his gallery and elsewhere.

Portrait of Hedda Nova (Mrs. Paul Hurst) (detail), c. 1920
Oil on canvas, 34 x 23 inches
Courtesy of Michael Johnson Fine Arts

The Stendahl Galleries hostess, Mildred Lawrence, also found herself a subject of the artist's brush. She had "tact, charm, unlimited patience, and moreover she was very good looking," as Kleitsch's fine portrait of her proves, confirming a certain seductive power he had over women. In the 1922 portrait (p. 81), Lawrence sports a popular flapper hairstyle of finger waves, and she is wearing glass beads, the style of the day. She wears a cover-up so that her dress will not get wrinkled or stained during the messy process of executing the finger waves with gel and water. In 1929, Lawrence left the gallery after her marriage to Allen Green, "leaving the patrons inconsolable" (Antony Anderson, *South Coast News*, January 25, 1929).

The years from 1921 to 1925 were exceedingly productive for Kleitsch, as he and his family explored the Southland and its natural wonders and took an extended motor trip to Northern California. With his restless nature, his perceptive eye, and his appetite for color, he was rewarded with countless opportunities and subjects to paint and record. For instance, he depicted his

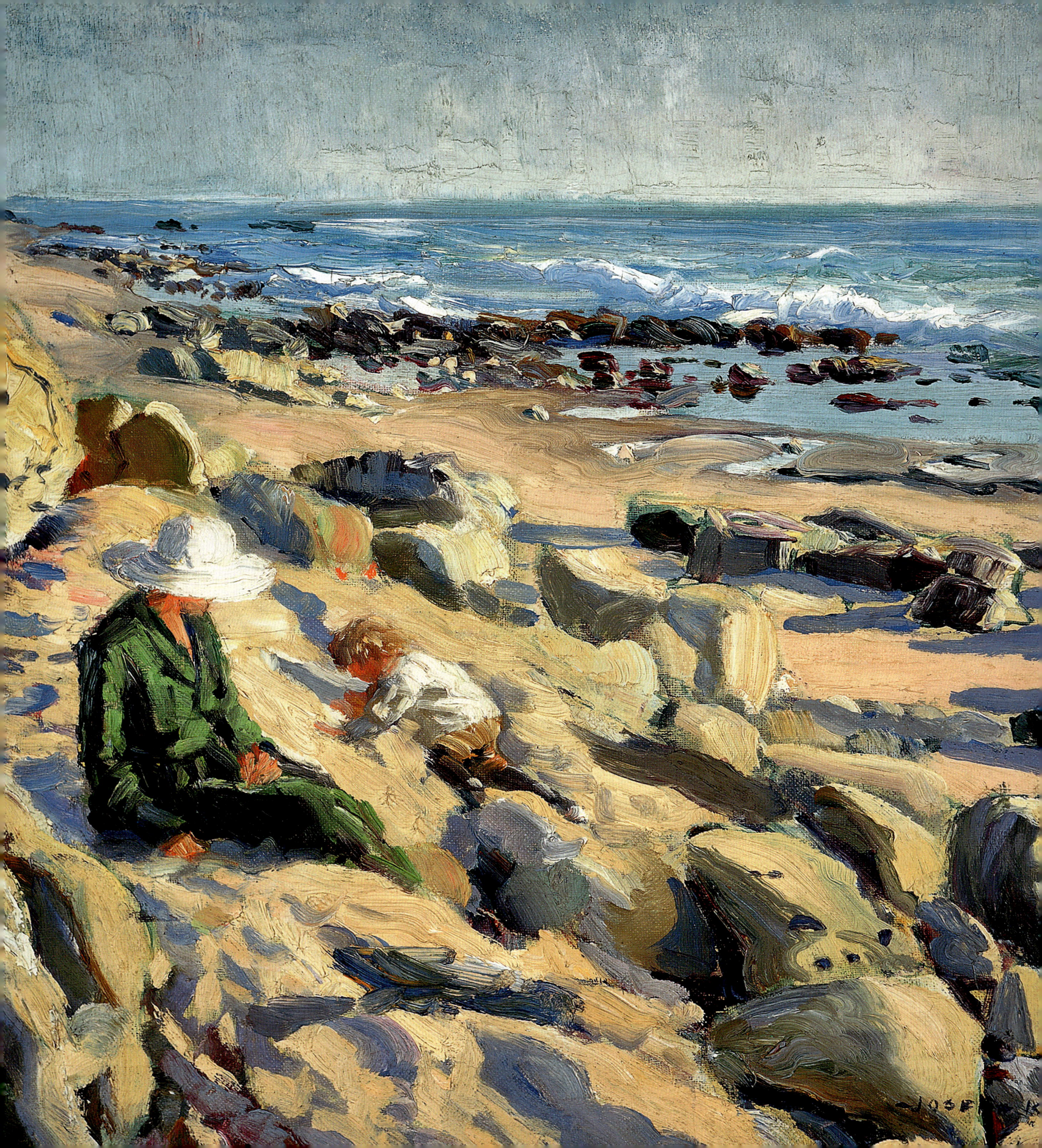

young son, Eugene, and his wife Edna frolicking on the sandy shores near Laguna's main beach. *Rocky Cliffs* (c. 1920–21) demonstrates his facility with impressionistic brushstrokes and blond tonalities while capturing the glaring, brilliant California sunlight. Despite his busy schedule, Kleitsch managed to take time off for leisure activities; during the summer months, he performed as a flutist in Laguna artist Isaac Frazee's Indian Pageant Play of the Peace Pipe and played Hungarian melodies on the accordion for Frank Adams' "Circus." The Kleitsches were involved in Laguna's social life and community activities, and they enjoyed hosting dinners and informal games in the artist's studio, as evidenced by *Highlights*.

Kleitsch began to use decorative patterns and vivid chromatic effects as early as 1918, as shown in the painting *Problematicus* (p. 55), and this tendency became more pronounced in his California paintings. Christian Brinton, an art critic, characterized Hungarian painting as follows in his review of the Panama-Pacific Exposition of 1916 in San Francisco: "The art of Hungary is before all else a typically rhapsodic expression. . . . In each [artwork] you meet the same deep-rooted race spirit, the same love of vivid chromatic effect, the same fervid lyric passion" (*Impressions of the Art at the Panama-Pacific Exposition*, 1916). Kleitsch's *The Oriental Shop* (p. 65), *Laguna Road* (p. 37), *Highlights*, and several other California paintings illustrate the artist's awakened sensitivity and understanding of the application of color.

Rocky Cliffs, Laguna (Edna and Eugene)
(detail), c. 1920–21
Oil on canvas, 18 x 20 inches
Private Collection, from the
Estate of Pearl Martin

The artist's transition from portraiture to lyrical and colorful interpretations of the landscape of Laguna Beach was recognized in an exhibition review by art critic Vandyke Brown: "You never dreamt [that this 'uncompromising belligerent with the broad brush' could offer] a diversity in composition and subject hard to beat anywhere else" (*Life and Art*, July 28, 1922). The display of thirty-eight of Kleitsch's works showed "infinite beauty of the gamut of colors" (*Laguna Life*, August 4, 1922).

Kleitsch was also captivated by the picturesque architecture and setting of Mission San Juan Capistrano, and he frequently painted the mission and its environs. The artist often enlivened these canvases with figures of different ethnic backgrounds engaged in various activities. The painting *Curiosity* pictures two girls who are curious about the artist's paint box and palette, an enchanting moment that Kleitsch was able to capture on canvas (p. 113). The workmen engaged in restoring the mission did not escape his attention and found themselves as subjects for several of his pictures. El Peón, a plasterer, sat for his portrait (p. 109) and was also pictured in *The Story Teller,* while amusing Kleitsch's son, Eugene, with wild tales of the mission (p. 111). These paintings from Kleitsch's passionate toils came to be recognized by art critics and patrons as some of the most brilliant and spiritually moving of his new works with this focus.

With his increasing exposure through exhibitions and his critical acclaim, Kleitsch gained many sales for his landscapes and for his portraits. With this financial success, he was able to move to a larger residence in Laguna, and he purportedly purchased a lot for a house and future studio at Legion and Through streets. Due to the success of his exhibitions, the Kleitsches were able to move into a new residence in Los Angeles, and they began dividing their time between the city and Laguna.

Altar Boy (detail), n.d.
Oil on canvas, 27 x 22 inches
The Irvine Museum

While residing in the city, Kleitsch worked with several of his artist friends to found the Painters and Sculptors Club of Los Angeles in July 1923. Their first meeting was held at the Ambassador Hotel studio that Stendahl had strategically arranged for Kleitsch, located in one of the Ambassador towers. Their objective was to form a democratic working club that would provide a studio with live models, where the artist members could draw or paint. It was modeled after the Palette and Chisel Club of Chicago and the Salmagundi Club of New York; it also included associate memberships for businessmen, who could mingle with the artists and models at social mixers and provide much-needed funding for the club. Additional funds came from exhibitions and auctions of small artworks donated by the artists.

Kleitsch continued his travels to San Juan Capistrano for extended sketching trips. The riotous, vibrant colors seen in the artist's figurative paintings now appeared in his landscape paintings as well. A strikingly beautiful painting titled *Red and Green* (1923, p. 107) exemplifies his response to this environment. Edna, wearing her familiar red jacket, shades her eyes as a youthful Mexican girl kneels nearby among the flowering plants and a large, leafy pepper tree. In this painting, the artist lends a sense of deeper religious significance to the mission's faded grandeur and tranquility.

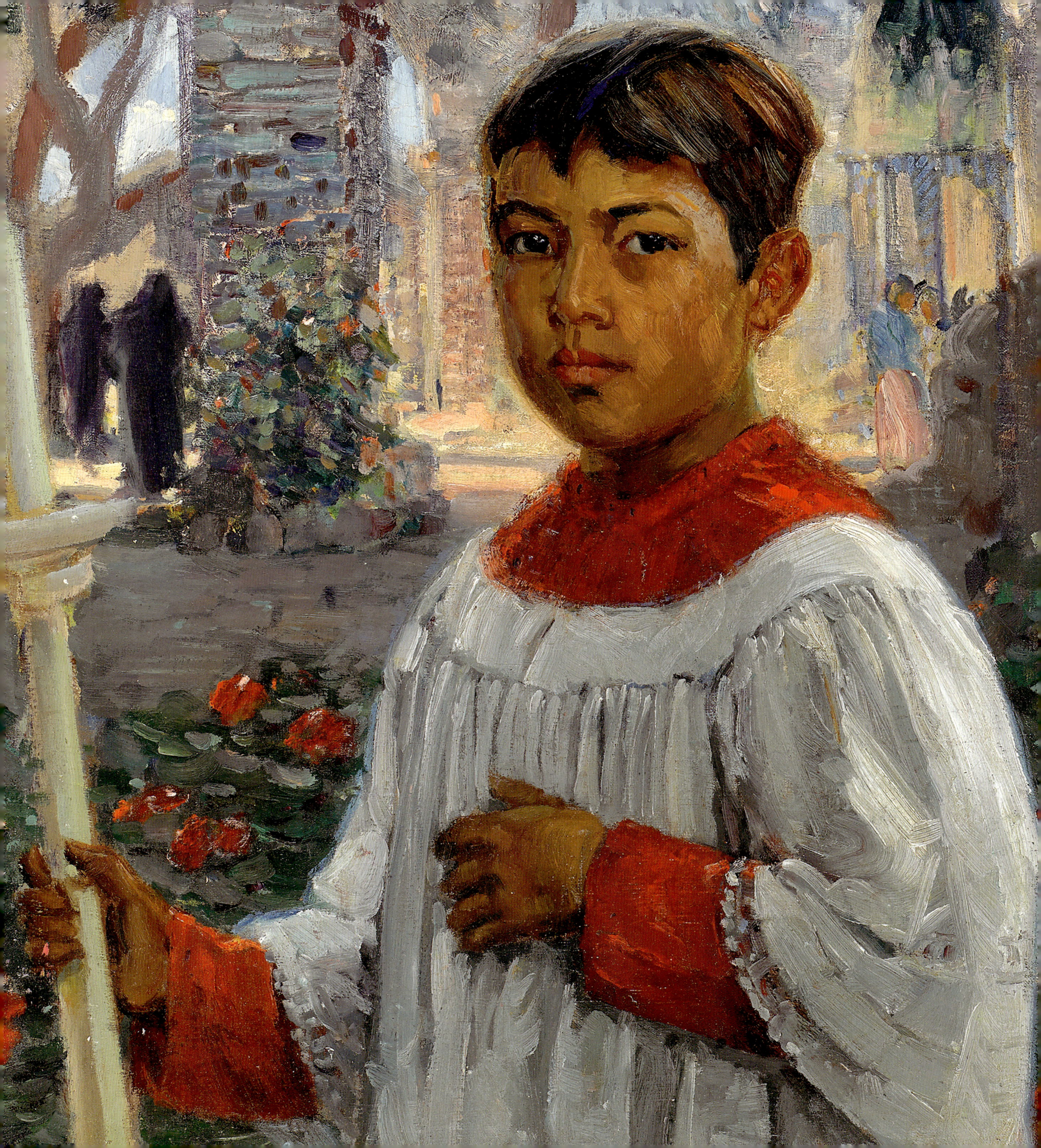

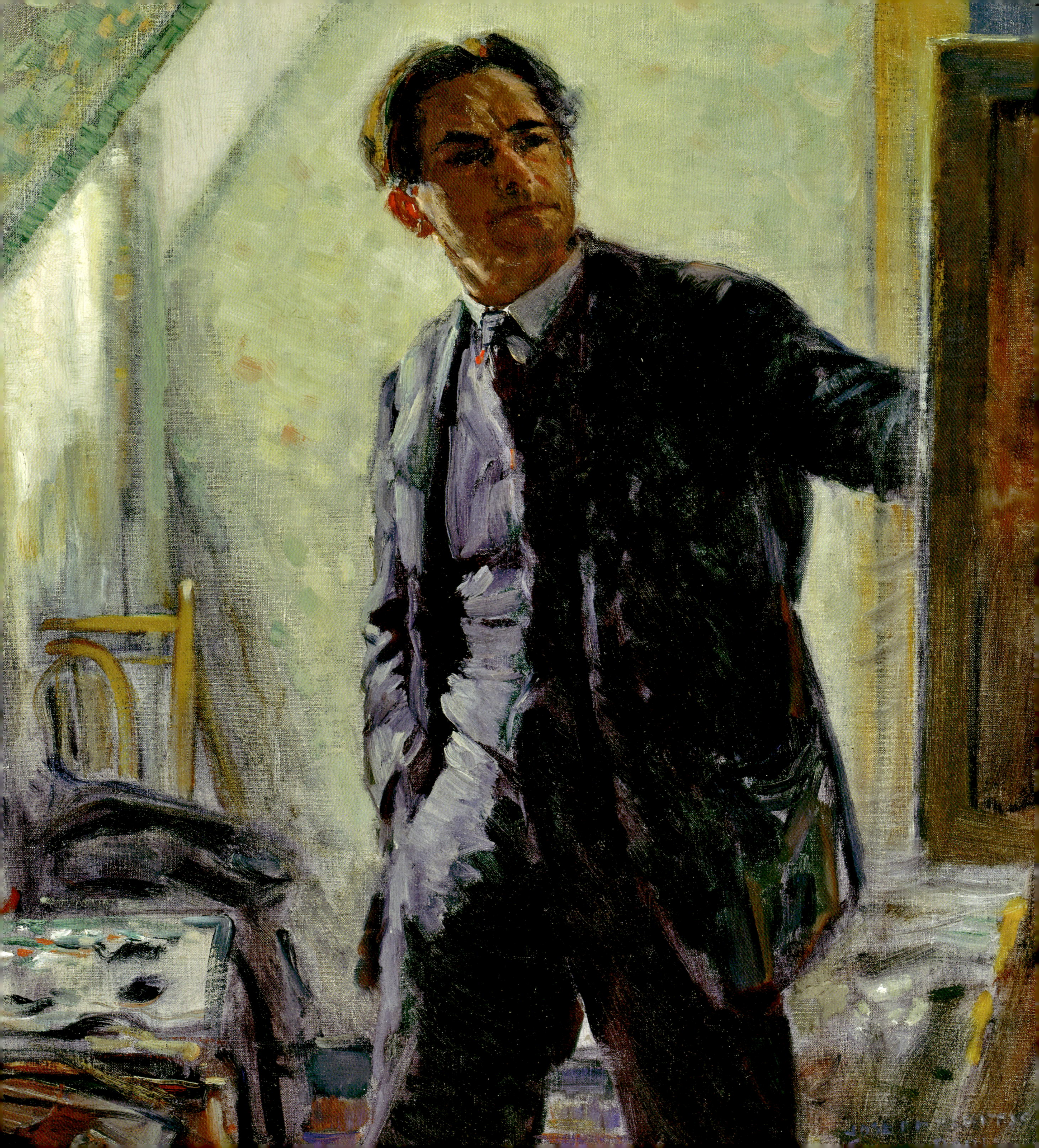

During 1923 and 1924, the artist painted a prodigious number of scenes of Old Laguna. His vigorous brush, loaded with myriad rich colors and manipulating the ever-changing light, effectively captured the mood of the old village. Antony Anderson wrote, "Joseph Kleitsch is a true artist, ever on the alert for the new word in any manifestation of nature, and with an exquisite responsiveness to its meaning to him, the interpreter." Although Anderson was effusive in his praise, he maintained that Kleitsch's portraits and figure pictures "still remained his finer and stronger works" (*Los Angeles Times*, October 28, 1923). Somewhat later, the artist's dynamic, brilliant landscapes and marinescapes would prove Anderson wrong.

In December 1924, the *Carmel Pine Cone* reported that Kleitsch was painting in Carmel for the winter season. The paintings that remain from this trip convincingly show the difference between the climates of Northern and Southern California, manifesting less enchantment for the gray, overcast skies and cold climate of the north. Kleitsch declared the region a "trifle cold for his temperament." Edna, who enjoyed hiking and wandering the high cliffs among the pines, agreed with him that Laguna offered a better environment, with its vivid colors and brilliant light for painting.

Self-Portrait, Paris (detail), 1926
Oil on canvas, 18 x 15 inches
Collection of Brent Gross

The year 1925 was a banner one for the artist, as he anticipated a trip to Europe in October and dealt with a demanding exhibition schedule and a number of portrait commissions. He was installed as vice president of the Painters and Sculptors Club and also served on the model committee; given his eye for attractive women, he was perfect for the role. During this time, he painted several exuberant and colorful still lifes displaying a profusion of antique Asian objects. These items belonged to the G. T. Marsh and Company gift shop in the Ambassador Hotel, where Kleitsch had painted *The Oriental Shop* (p. 65) with Florence Marsh and his wife Edna.

Before he left for Europe, Kleitsch painted the portrait of Edward B. Good, an industrialist from Lancaster, Ohio, who was a strong supporter of the artist and possibly financed his trip. At the time and into 1931, the artist was still pursuing portraiture as his principal source of income. Among his many portraits were those of artist William Griffith's son Nelson (1922); Mrs. Bea Frank, the Ambassador Hotel manager's wife (1925); and Ruth E. Bach (1930). Surprisingly, some critics complained about the highly mannered and less individual expression of these sitters.

Up until the date of his departure, Kleitsch was involved in exhibitions and commissions, and he had little personal time for himself and his family. He had immigrated to the United States thirteen years earlier, and he now felt a need to broaden his career and vision by travel and further European study; Stendahl favored this scheme and planned to join him in 1926.

On his way to the port of embarkation, Kleitsch stopped with his family in Chicago, where he was feted by his colleagues and given a reception by patrons, collectors, old friends, and relatives. The Kleitsches then traveled to Grand Rapids, Michigan, home to Edna's family and the place where she had lived as a child. They stayed at the Rowe Hotel, the social center of the city, projecting an image of the artist's success to the locals. While there, Kleitsch painted a unique self-portrait (p. 135) in a landscape setting unlike that of his previous paintings, a move that could be interpreted as the beginning of a change in his career path. His maturity and confidence are self-evident in this portrait, which depicts him as a successful practitioner of the arts.

Ancient and Modern Normandie, Vernon, France (detail), 1926
Oil on canvas, 36 x 40 inches
Private Collection

The artist's passport, issued on January 21, 1926, gives pertinent information about the Kleitsches' stay in New York City, where they made the decision that Edna should remain in the States with their son, whose schooling was of primary importance to both; undoubtedly, financial issues were also of some consideration. The artist left for Europe on the SS *President Roosevelt* on February 6. On February 14, Edna reported to Stendahl that her husband had arrived in Paris, where an important commission awaited him. The artist began frequenting the bistros of Montparnasse, where gatherings of intellectuals and artists also attracted a covey of Parisian women. Kleitsch's reputation as a rogue was validated by the number of unidentified women he painted while traveling alone in Europe, and this was confirmed by certain members of his family. Most probably, these character studies were motivated more by excess of libido than by professional concerns. One such portrait he called "*Oui*" because, as he said, like "all French girls, she has a prettily pursed mouth that is shaped from saying *oui* so often and so smilingly."

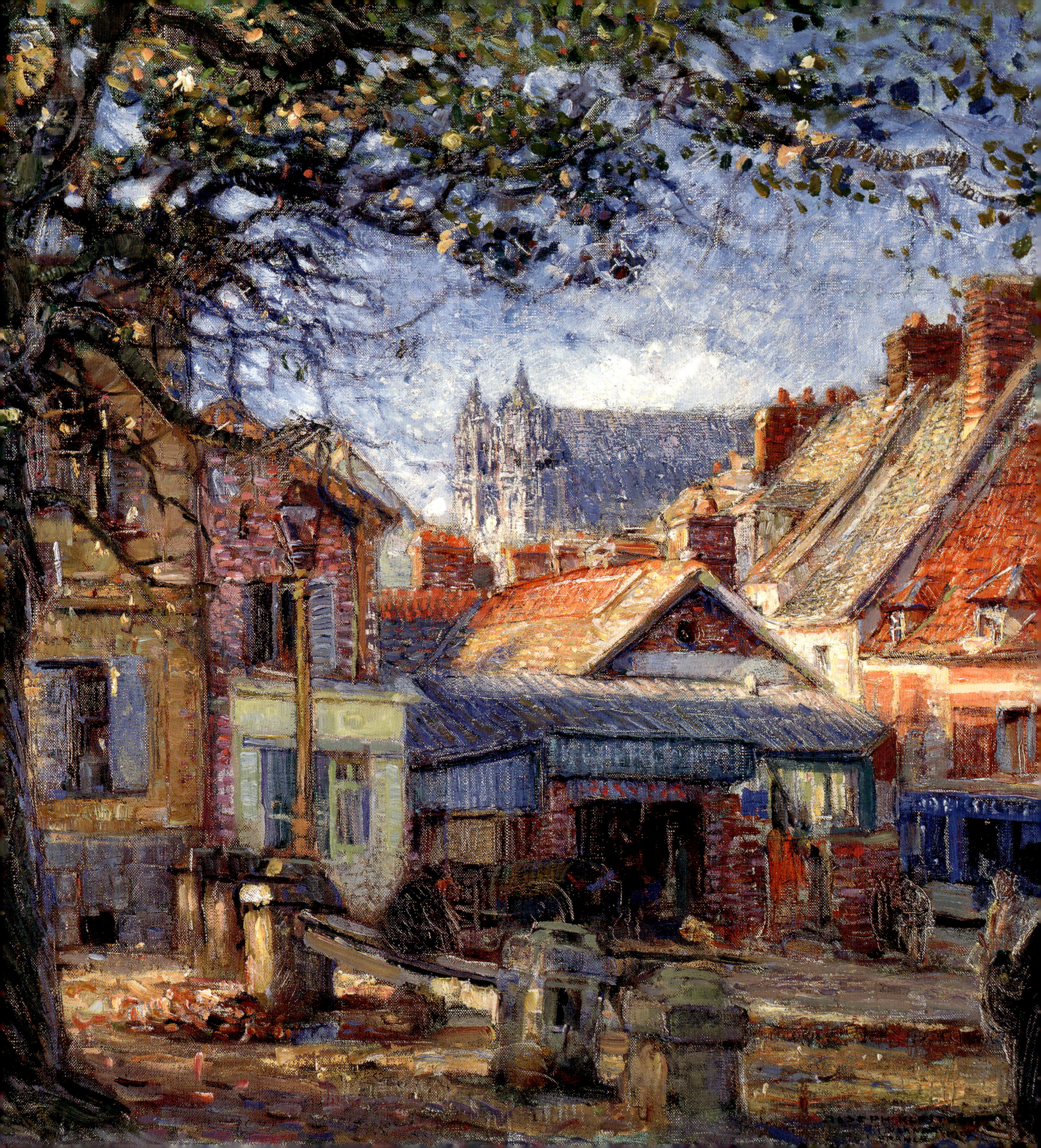

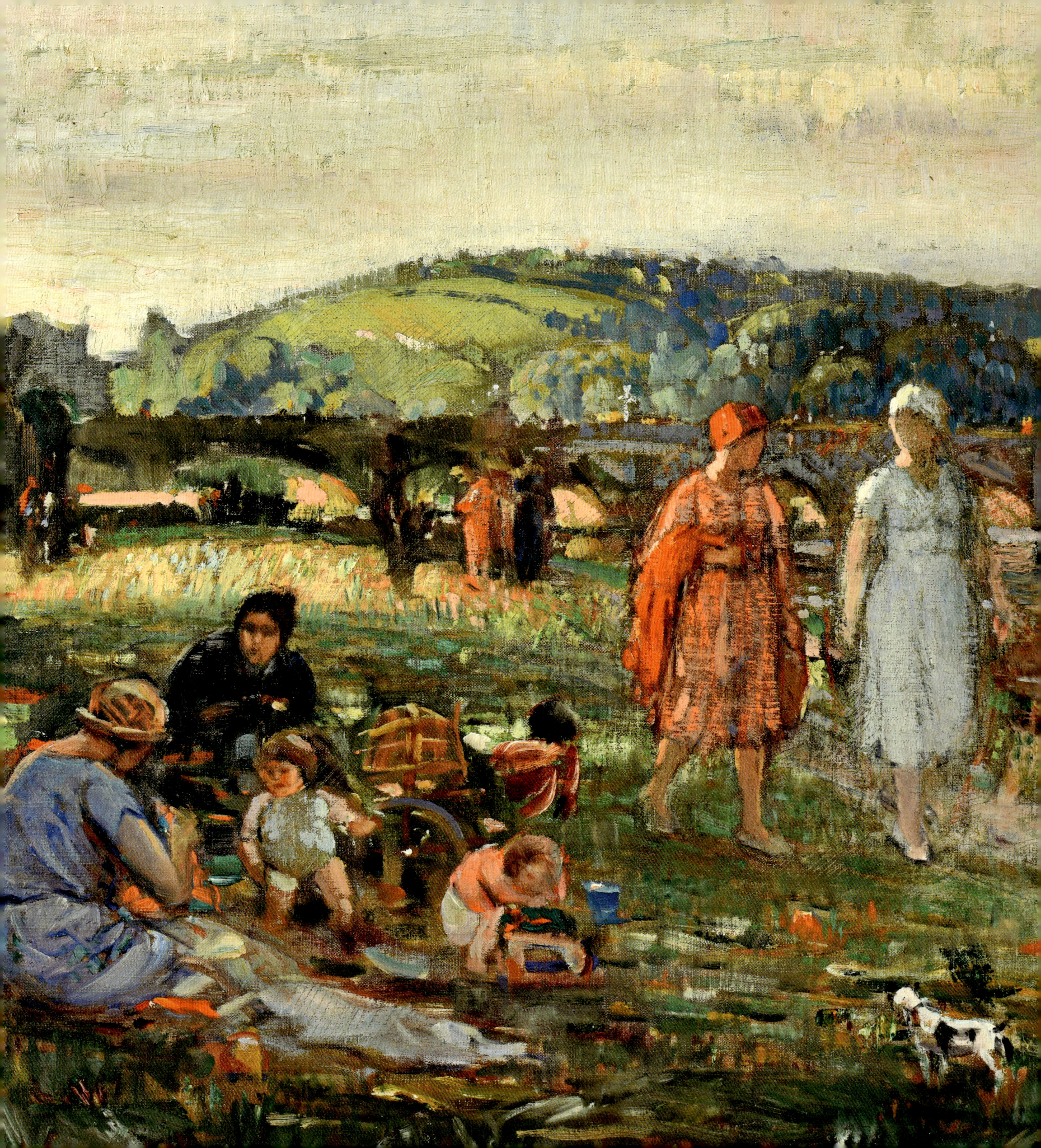

The next stop on his journey was Madrid, where he spent many hours at the Prado Museum, admiring and studying the Old Masters, especially Titian (c. 1488–1576) and Diego Velázquez (1599–1660), both of whom he had always respected. The influence of these artists is reflected in several of Kleitsch's Chicago portraits that were singled out by art critics.

Kleitsch also visited Asturias, in northern Spain, where he was commissioned to paint the portraits of several of his former patrons, like the Wades, who had purchased fifteen of his paintings during the artist's second trip to Mexico in 1911–12. He then traveled to Seville, where he painted in the gardens of the Alcázar and witnessed the gorgeous pageantry of the Nazarene processions during Holy Week. Unfortunately, very few paintings from this visit have surfaced to date.

When Kleitsch returned to Paris, he had no specific plans or agenda but, fortuitously, met a fellow American artist, Abel George Warshawsky (1883–1962), an avid impressionist painter from Cleveland, Ohio, who now resided in Paris. Warshawsky related his vivid observations of Vernon and Giverny, located in Normandy. Kleitsch was inspired by Warshawsky's enthusiasm for the village of Vernon, located just across the Seine from Giverny, which Warshawsky thought "seemed cramped and overcultivated" by the lure of Monet. In June 1926, Kleitsch joined the artist and two of his friends on a trip to both villages. They settled at the old Hôtel Soleil d'Or, where Kleitsch was introduced to the proprietor's blond daughter, Simone; not surprisingly, he produced a painting that portrays her natural loveliness.

Lunch Hour, Vernon, France (detail), 1926
Oil on canvas, 18 x 21 inches
Collection of Donald Buehler

Vernon, unlike Giverny, still retained an atmosphere of simplicity and tranquility, which reminded the artist of his native Hungary. Warshawsky's impressionistic paintings inspired Kleitsch to do more work in that mode. Stimulated by the countryside, Kleitsch also painted a number of fine canvases with a more poetic feeling. *Lunch Hour* and *Bathers along the Seine* (p. 125) are spontaneous studies with vibrant colors, showing everyday activity along the river bank. In both, the artist employed short, broken brushstrokes and soft colors, moving toward a more impressionistic painting style.

Stendahl joined Kleitsch from mid-July to mid-October, and the two of them traveled together throughout Europe, visiting Munich, Rome, Florence, Vienna, and Budapest, as well as cities in Romania and England. When they were not viewing works in exhibitions and galleries or enjoying the fruits of European cuisine, the artist painted incessantly, in an almost orgiastic outburst of energy. Stendahl wrote to Kleitsch later that year, "I don't care what you do or how much, just plant yourself and paint . . . finish up enough stuff for a big exhibition." Unfortunately, nothing immediately came of Stendahl's offer, and most of the artist's productivity in Europe had to wait until 1928, when Stendahl gave Kleitsch a large and successful exhibition at his gallery.

In Paris, Kleitsch painted extensively the activity along the quays and below the bridges, which had fascinated artists for generations; he likewise portrayed the colorful Luxembourg Gardens, the Tuileries, and the Place du Carrousel. He also completed several richly painted figurative pictures, such as *Madonna and the Apples* and two versions of *Blue Thread* (p. 119). Velázquez had painted portraits of women sewing, and these seem to have been Kleitsch's inspiration for *Blue Thread*. A still life titled *Peonies* and an interior scene titled *Reflections* (p. 121) seem to have been inspired by Manet. Kleitsch also apparently noted the works of such artists as Monet, Matisse, and Cézanne, and these would influence his own future works.

Madonna and the Apples, Paris (detail), 1927
Oil on canvas, 28 x 36 inches
Collection of John and Regina Rowe

To counter the frenetic pace and distractions of Paris, the artist left for the tranquility of Vernon in late spring of 1927. At this time, he also visited Giverny and, while there, painted its dewy green valleys and meadows and its rustic farmhouses. Rumors of his philandering and lifestyle had reached Edna, which prompted her to write to Stendahl in June, questioning Kleitsch's fidelity. Stendahl reassured her in a letter of June 1927 that Kleitsch was a "fine boy" and "much better than the average man." And, he stated, "I can see no reason why he should stay over in Europe any longer, as there is much work to be done here." Kleitsch was under the impression that Stendahl would rejoin him in Europe that year to arrange for a Paris exhibition, and he was disappointed when the dealer canceled his trip at the last minute. Greatly despondent, the artist told him he felt as though he "had been left alone in the world."

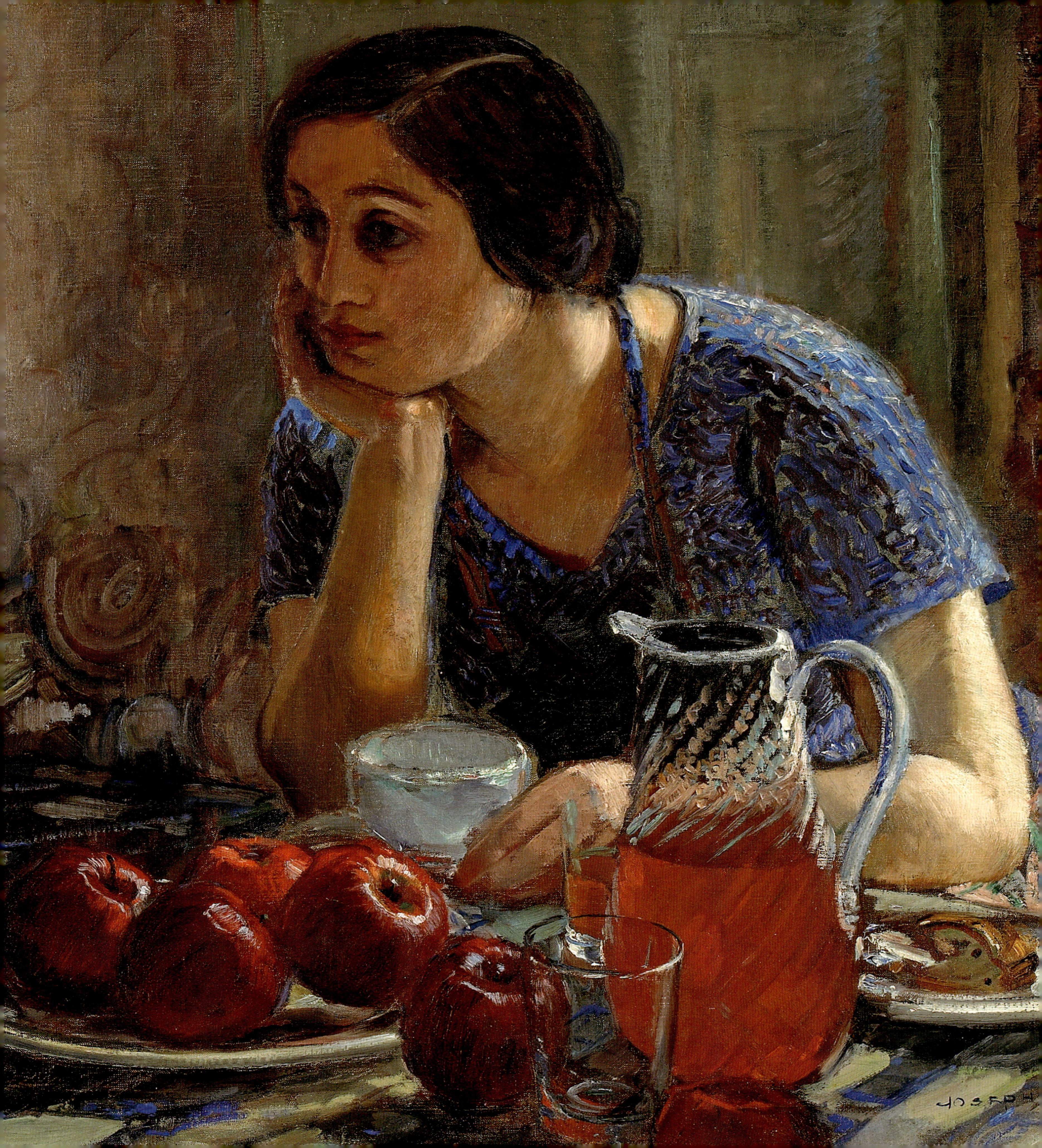
JOSEPH

Kleitsch returned to America in November 1927 to be reconciled with Edna; he promptly rented a large studio in the Athenaeum Building in Chicago to prepare for his "homecoming" show in Los Angeles. Stendahl insisted that Kleitsch have all his paintings there by January, in order to prepare for the publicity campaign. As promised by the dealer, the exhibition at the Stendahl Galleries was highly successful and received broad coverage by the local press. On May 13, *Los Angeles Times* critic Antony Anderson previewed the show and wrote, "Joseph Kleitsch has successfully slowed down his pace, taken more time for thoughtful design and refinement of color and paint application. . . .This is a first reflection on his 'Homecoming' exhibition at the Stendahl Galleries." Critic Fred Hogue wrote an article titled "An Hungarian Artist" in the *Los Angeles Times* on June 25, 1928, raving: "As I look at the canvases of Joseph Kleitsch I forget the painter. As a colorist he is not clever; he is great. If the mantle of Titian has fallen upon a modern artist, it is draped about the shoulders of this Hungarian painter.... Los Angeles is richer because the tropical bird of wonderful plumage has found a nest here."

Laguna Road (detail), 1924
Oil on canvas, 36 x 40 inches
Collection of the City of Laguna Beach

Amid his preparations for the 1928 exhibition, Kleitsch managed to paint several portraits, such as the one of the glamorous silent-movie actress Ruth Renick (p. 79); undoubtedly, these commissions were arranged by Stendahl to provide the artist with an immediate source of income.

In the meantime, changes were coming to Laguna. In January 1929, the town's first modern hostel, La Casa del Camino, announced that it would open on February 1, and the proprietor arranged for his friend Kleitsch to exhibit paintings of Old Laguna in the hotel lounge and dining room. Art critics proclaimed that these scenes were greatly prized by the artist, who attached sentimental value to them. Indeed, his art provides a conduit to the past before the spoliation of what he considered Laguna's pristine environment and small-town character. Kleitsch recognized Laguna's imminent transition from a village to an expanded urban center, with a multitude of new businesses. Through his paintings, Kleitsch was recognized as an early preservationist by his peers, art critics, and the media.

Toward the end of 1929 and the beginning of 1930, Kleitsch began to record the changes that marked this significant transition. His focus was now less

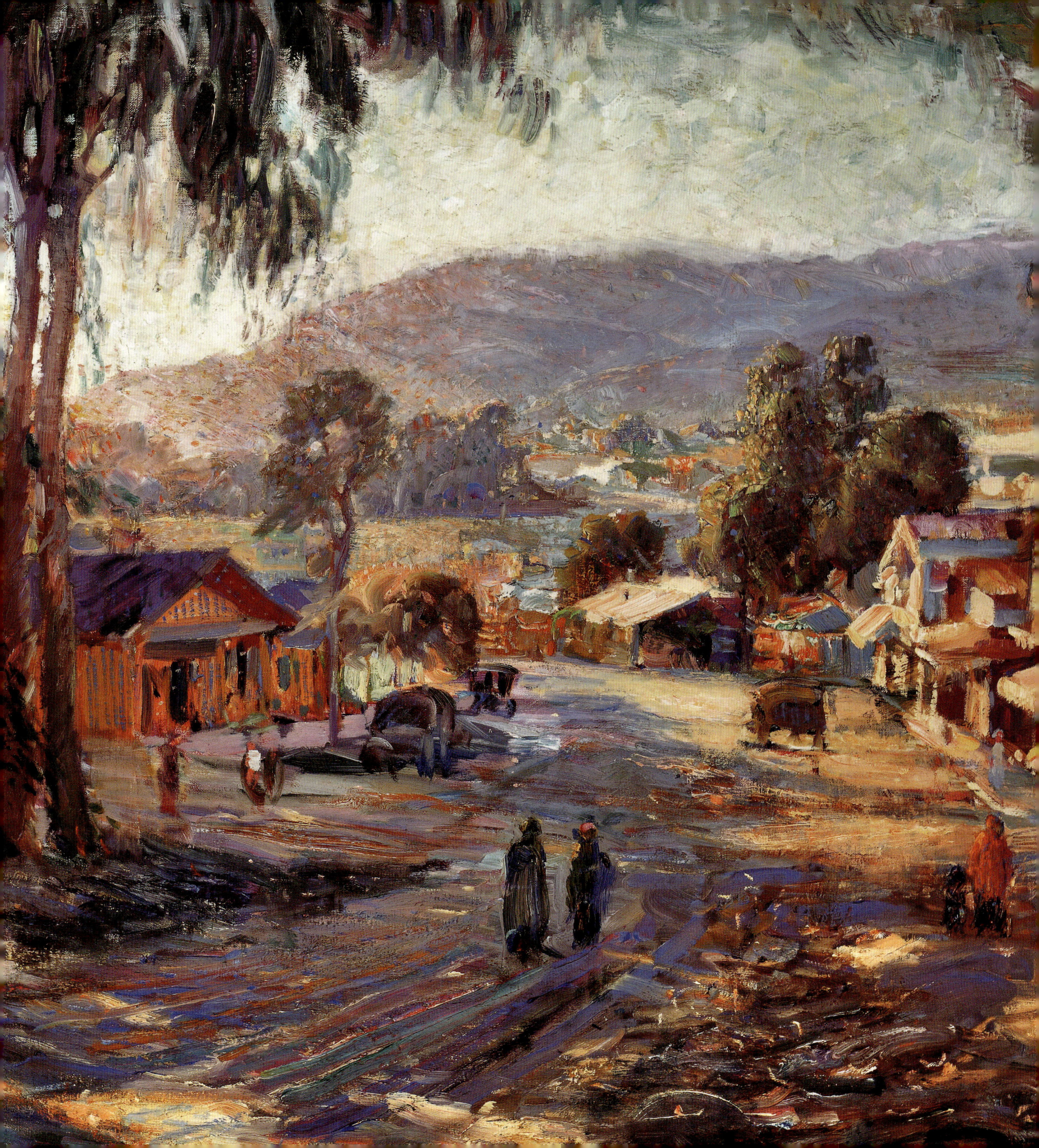

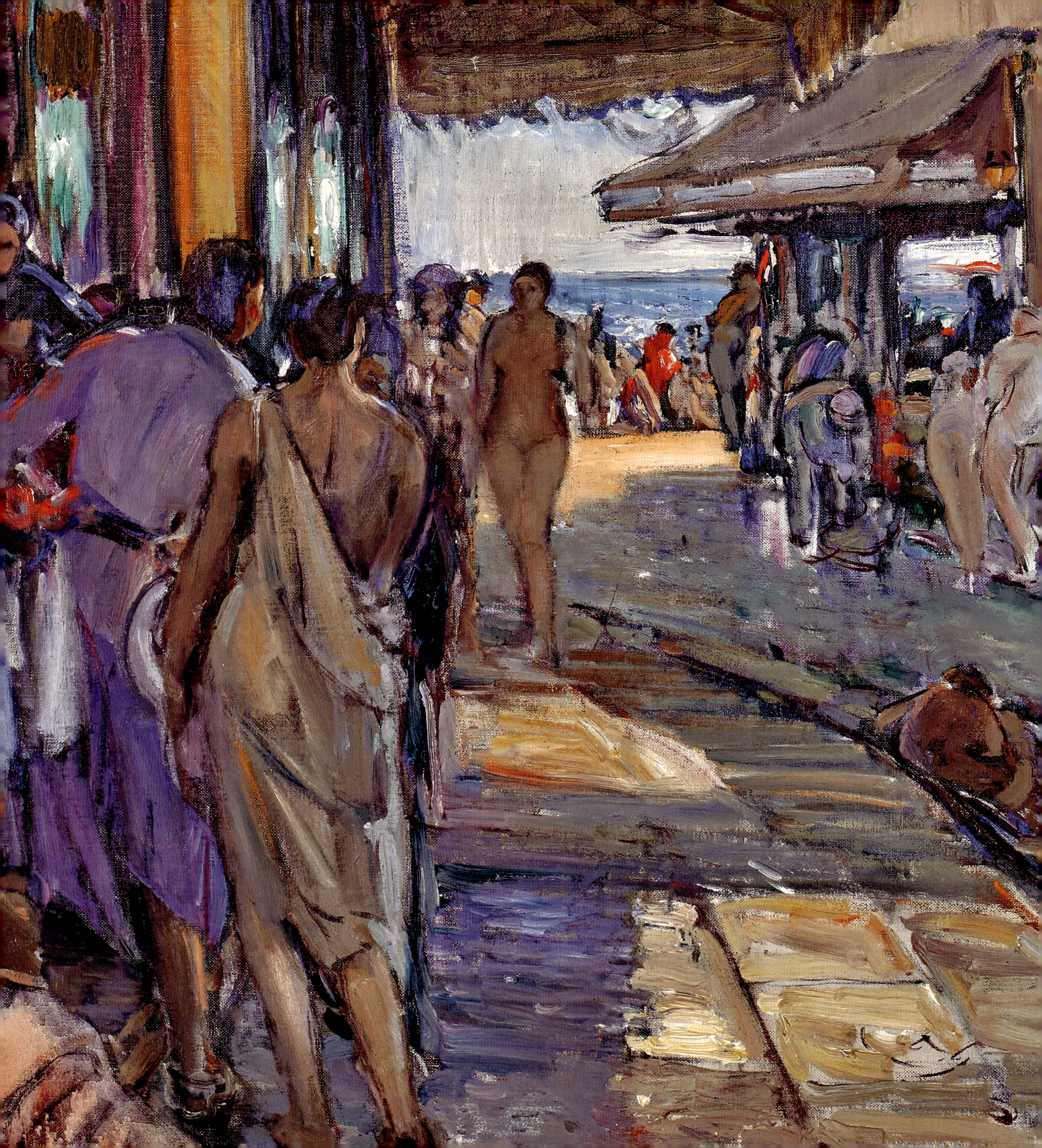

on portraiture and more on street scenes, with their beehive of activity—the people, cars, and buildings of the new downtown Laguna. Kleitsch's most captivating and ambitious compositions were those that captured the complex choreography of figures parading and mingling along the avenues and assembling at Main Beach. These figures were summarily notated, with no personal identity, only there to give a sense of reality: the abstracted, gestural figures convey movement and visual tension in these varied scenes.

Toward the end of his all-too-brief career, Kleitsch's artistry was changing from a mode of realism to an expressive style with the inclusion of abstract patterning. With this abstraction and broader, more abbreviated brushwork, the paintings indicate that the artist was increasingly adopting abstract strategies. The complexity of these late paintings sets him apart from many of the California plein-air painters of his day.

Though the Great Depression affected all facets of the Laguna community, the spirit of the arts continued to prevail, though on a limited basis. Undoubtedly, the climate and tranquility of the city of Laguna, with its seaside setting, gave it a significant advantage over America's larger cities. In spite of the bleakness of the economy in 1929, Kleitsch was still receiving portrait commissions and selling paintings. However, the stock market crash in October crippled the finances of most art collectors, causing his dealer, Stendahl, severe difficulty in collecting payments for paintings that had previously been sold. A serious rift developed between Kleitsch and Stendahl, with the artist requesting that the dealer return all of his paintings and frames and produce an itemized list and statement of all sales to date. Despite his lean finances, the artist was given an opportunity to purchase the old Yoch Catholic church in July 1931; he moved it to his property at Legion and Through streets to use as a studio, later slated to become the Kleitsch Academy of Fine Arts.

Ocean Front—Main Beach, Laguna (detail), c. 1929–30
Oil on canvas, 36 x 40 inches
Collection of Stephen P. Diamond, M.D.

Severe financial pressures and limited sales of paintings, along with Kleitsch's driven personality, contributed to his fatal heart attack on November 16, 1931. His premature death sparked an outpouring of tributes from friends, collectors, dealers, art critics, and the news media. In June 1933, a memorial exhibition was held in his honor at the Los Angeles Museum of History, Science, and Art in Exposition Park.

Kleitsch's legacy and extraordinary achievement in portraiture stems from his innate sensitivity to his subjects' individual expressions; this is especially discernable in non-commissioned portraits of sitters he knew well, as their individual visages and mannerisms were familiar to him. This acuity in representing the distinctive personalities of his sitters placed him in a prominent position among his peers.

As mentioned above, toward the end of his career, Kleitsch focused less on portraiture as a means to explore personal identity and more on the intricate interactions of abstracted, gestural figures summarily treated. If the artist had lived longer and continued moving in this pioneering direction, he may well have adopted a post-modern style and shifted away from realism and impressionism. However, owing to his untimely death, his achievements nearly slipped from public memory. Today he is remembered for his drive to develop creative innovations, his depth of feeling, his memorable portraits of a diversity of subjects, and his vivid depictions that resonate with not only aesthetic delight but also historical significance.

Patricia Trenton

Laguna on a Cloudy Day (Main Beach) (detail), c. 1930
Oil on canvas, 36 x 40 inches
Private Collection, From the Estate of Pearl Martin

Overleaf:
Problematicus (detail), 1918
Oil on canvas, 60 x 55 inches
Collection of Robert and Susan Ehrlich

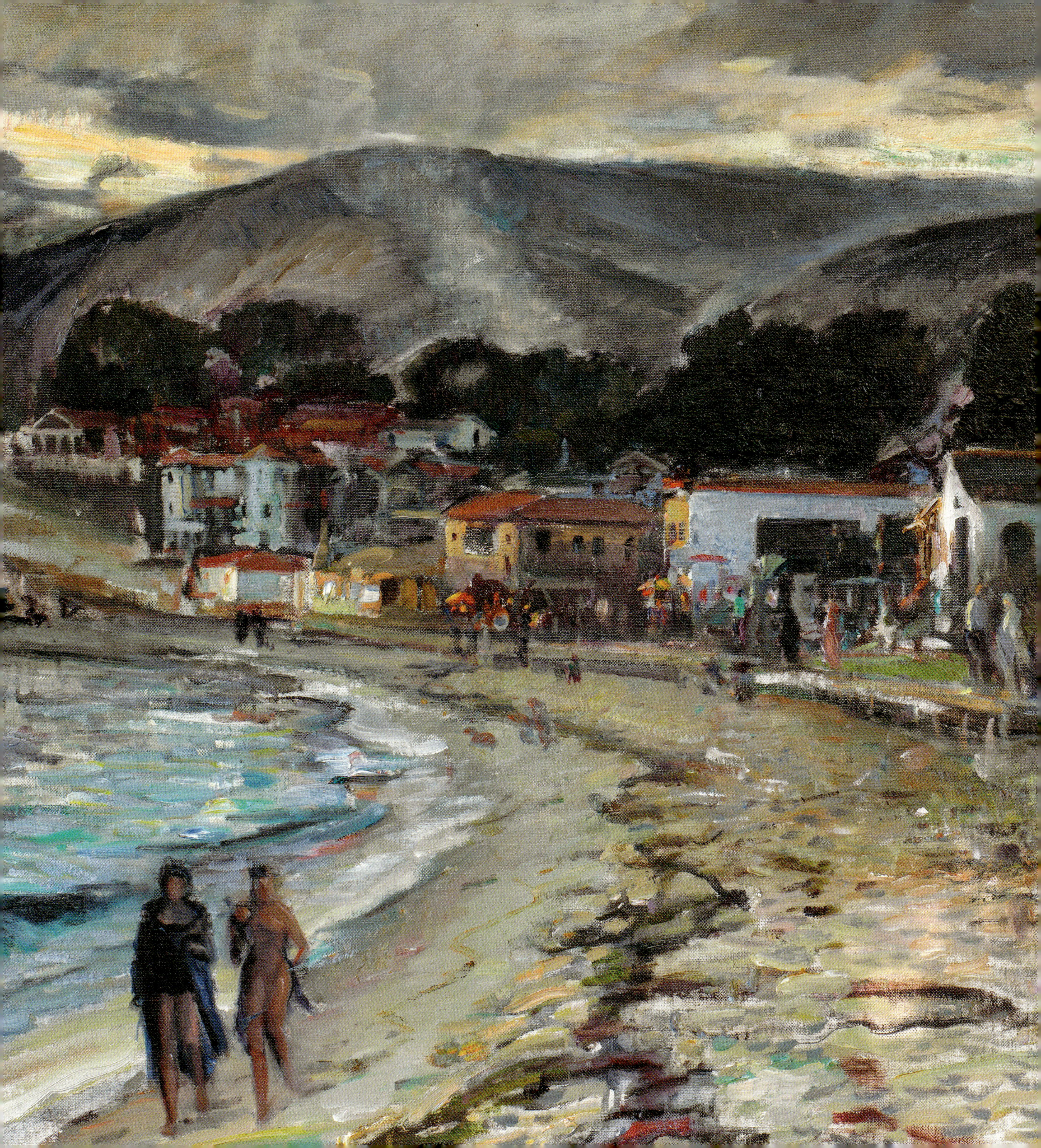

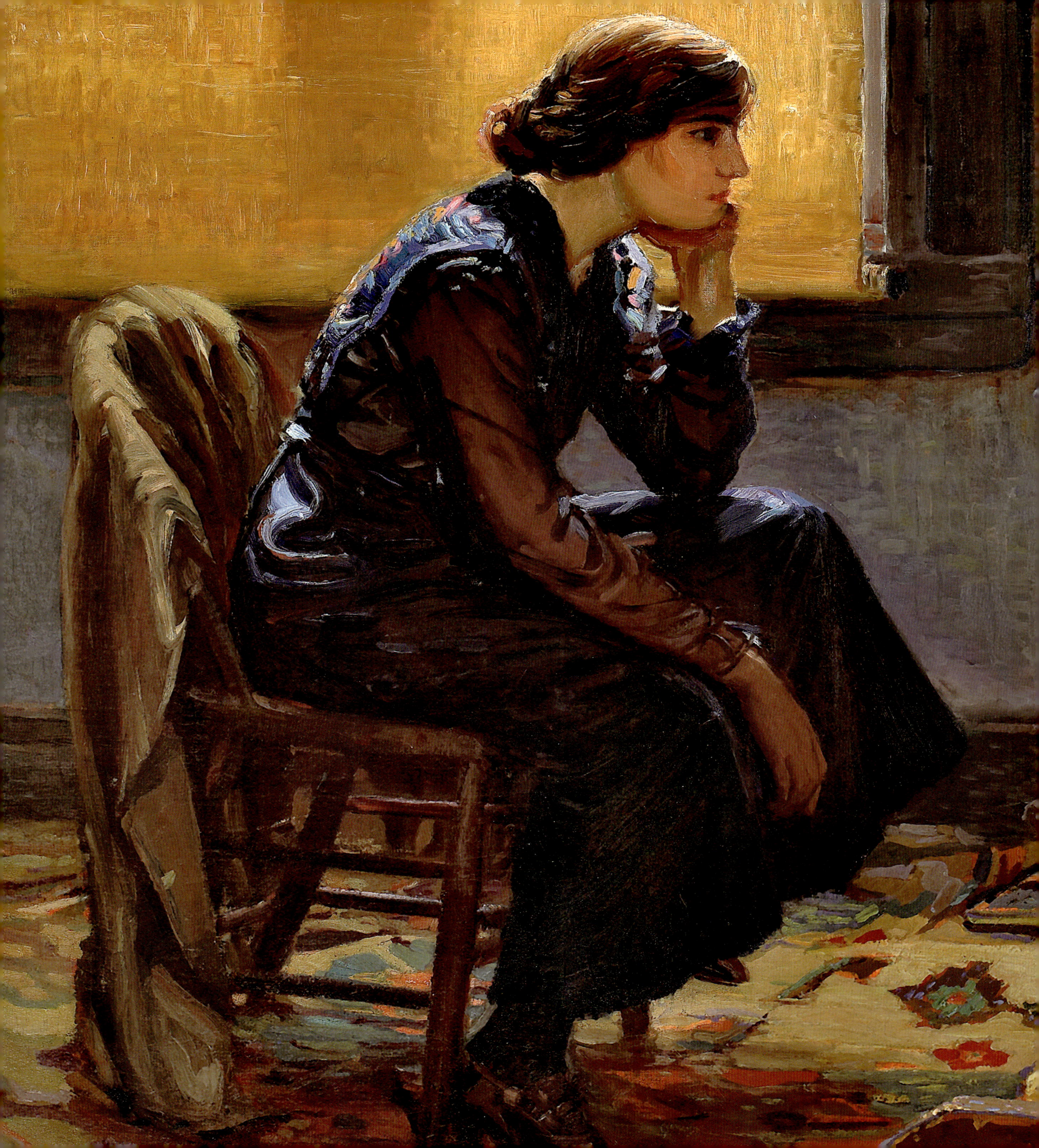

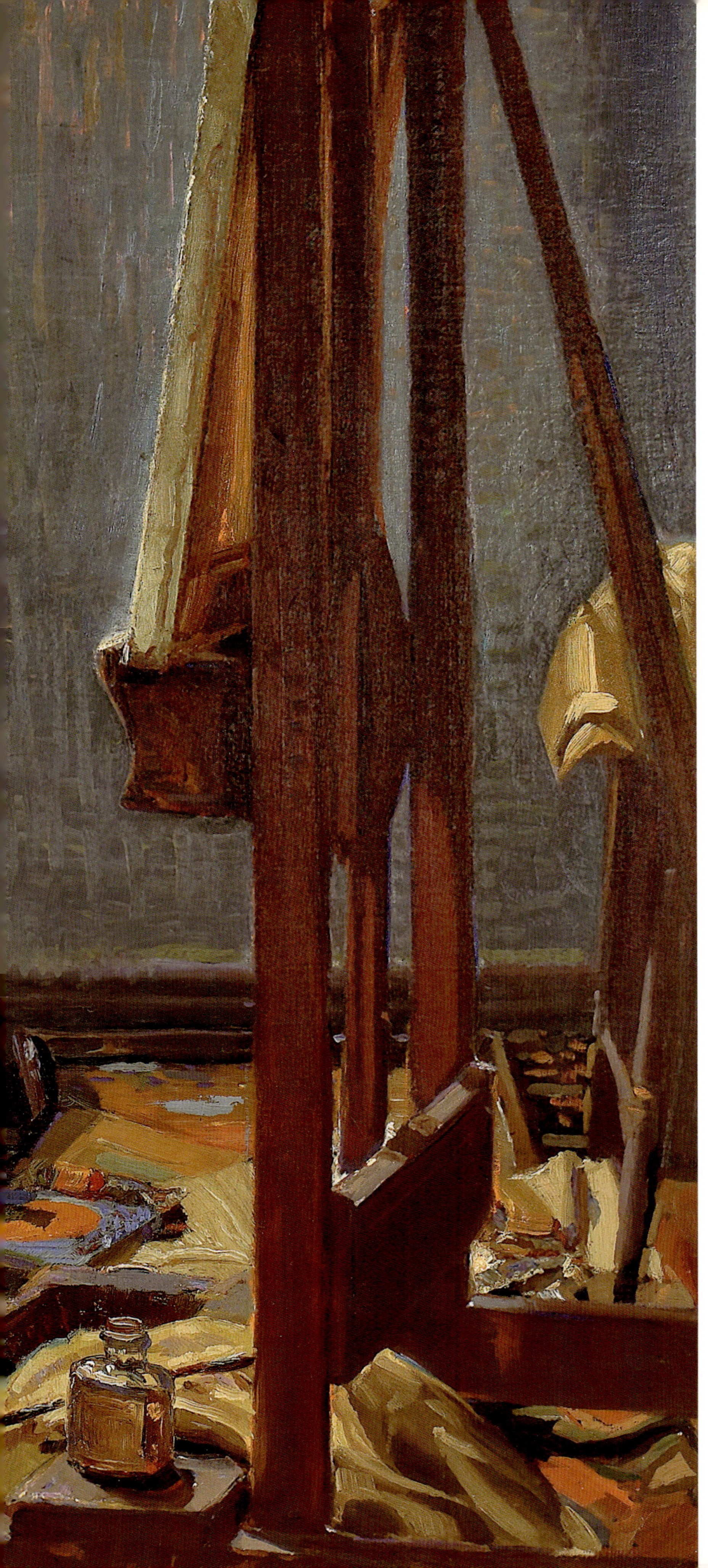

CATALOGUE

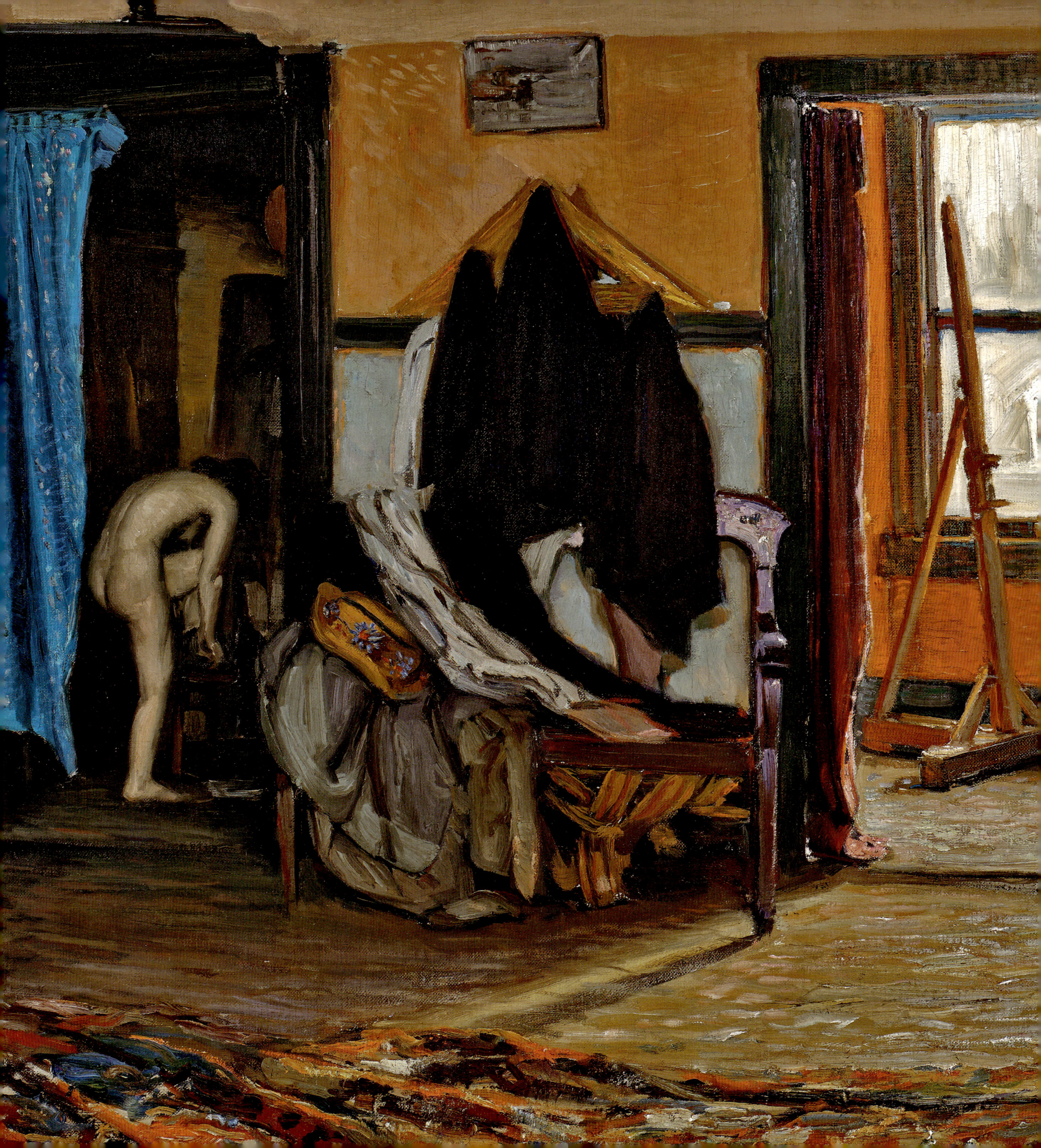

JOSEPH KLEITSCH'S KEEN SENSE of observation enabled him to capture an individual's demeanor and expression on canvas. He was unique among his peers for his bravura brushwork and for his ability to infuse the psychological nuances beneath outward appearances. The artist also relied on settings and props to help convey the status and personality of his sitters, similar to the traditional mode employed by the masterful expatriate artist John Singer Sargent (1856–1925). Poses and costumes were essential for rounding out Kleitsch's interpretations of the character of his subjects. In non-commissioned portrayals of friends and relatives, individual expression and freedom of thought and action are more discernible, such as in *The Attic Philosopher* (p. 53) and *Miss Ketchum* (p. 51). These spontaneously rendered portraits were of people he knew well; their mannerisms and personalities were more familiar, enabling him to personalize the paintings. Kleitsch's commissioned portraits, like the one of businessman Charles F. W. Nichols, are more formal and somewhat stiff, in keeping with the sitter's position in society. They do not reveal wrinkles, birthmarks, or unruly hairstyles, but portray a positive and successful image. After all, the patrons were paying hard dollars, and they expected artistic value for their money. By contrast, the non-commissioned portraits usually show the sitters in a more relaxed mood; for instance, Kleitsch's close male friends are usually pictured smoking or holding cigars, an accepted convention for male portraiture at the time.

A number of the portraits that Kleitsch painted in his studio at the Athenaeum Building in Chicago incorporate certain accessories, like antique rugs and furniture, along with an attractive arrangement of mellow light and rich shade, reflecting the Dutch influence on his art. Since the Athenaeum also provided unidentified models for his paintings, he created genre scenes rather than portraits. Though models are still used today, portraiture has become almost a vanishing art, as the camera and the computer have expanded the variety and use of reproductions. In a more contemporary vein, the plastic surgeon has served as an expensive means to improve and maintain a more youthful and dynamic persona for reproduction.

The following catalogue entries provide highlights of Kleitsch's innovative approach to portraiture. They are arranged in the following subject groupings: Studio Portraits and Genre Scenes; Laguna, New and Old; Mission San Juan Capistrano; Sojourn in Europe; and Self-Portraits. The sequence of paintings within these groupings is arranged by aesthetic association and occasionally by date.

Studio Interior (detail), c. 1915
Oil on canvas, 30 x 40 inches
Collection of Simon K. Chiu

THE ARTIST'S WIFE, 1919

Oil on canvas, 62 ¼ x 52 inches
Collection of Simon K. Chiu

THERE IS LITTLE INFORMATION about Kleitsch's artistic pursuits in 1913, but several events did occur that changed the course of his life and career: his first wife Emma's sudden death, from the complications of nephritis, in Chicago on August 10, and his new acquaintance that fall with Edna Gregaitis, an art teacher in the Chicago public schools. It was a significant transition, from a wife twenty-five years his senior to an attractive woman eight years his junior. On December 4 of the same year, the artist was approved for membership in the Palette and Chisel Club of Chicago, and he became actively involved in the club's numerous activities, broadening both his artistic and social agendas.

The courtship with Edna blossomed, and on July 22, 1914, they were married in Chicago in a civil ceremony performed by a judge, even though both had embraced Catholicism; why they chose a civil ceremony instead of a religious one is a real-life conundrum. One year later, their son, Eugene, was born. To celebrate the birth of their son, in 1916, Kleitsch painted a striking portrait of Edna, employing an impressionistic technique and a blond palette (p. 20). Kleitsch with loving care has crafted his wife's portrait to subtly reveal her beauty and exquisite facial features—her mouth, dark eyes, and high cheekbones. The placement of the sitter near a window, to illuminate both the figure and the room, brings out the sheen of Edna's satin dress and the glow of her face and hands. This was an experimental technique for the artist, as he distanced himself from his usual realistic mode of representation.

With much success, Kleitsch continued to paint half- and full-length portraits of himself and his wife in various attitudes and dress. In 1919, he painted a stunning full-length portrait of Edna, titled *The Artist's Wife.* In the June 1919 *Fine Arts Journal,* critic William Pattison wrote a laudatory article about Kleitsch's art. Pattison was obviously impressed with the monumental and elegant portrait of the artist's wife. He admired her pretty, "smooth round

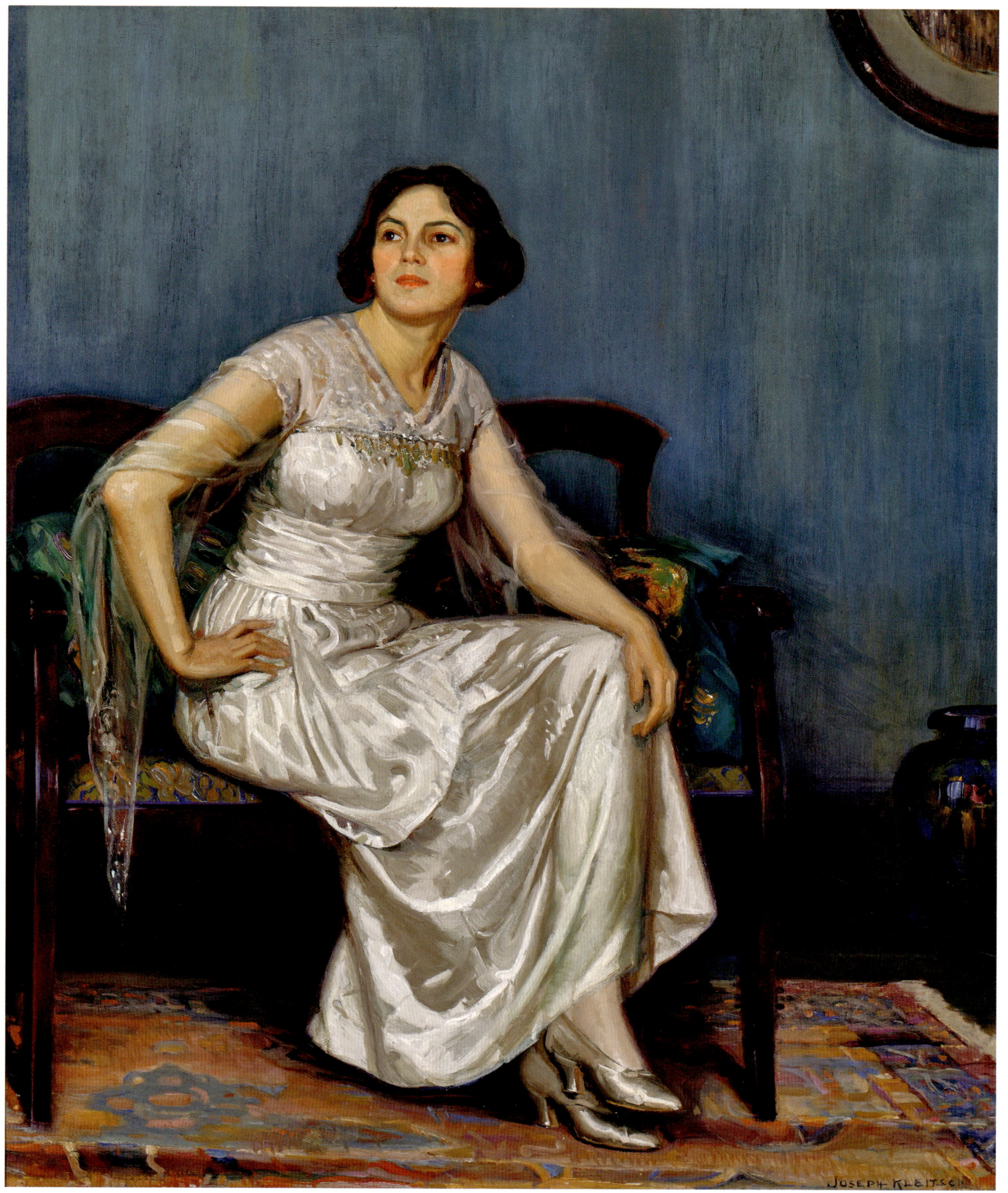
JOSEPH KLEITSCH

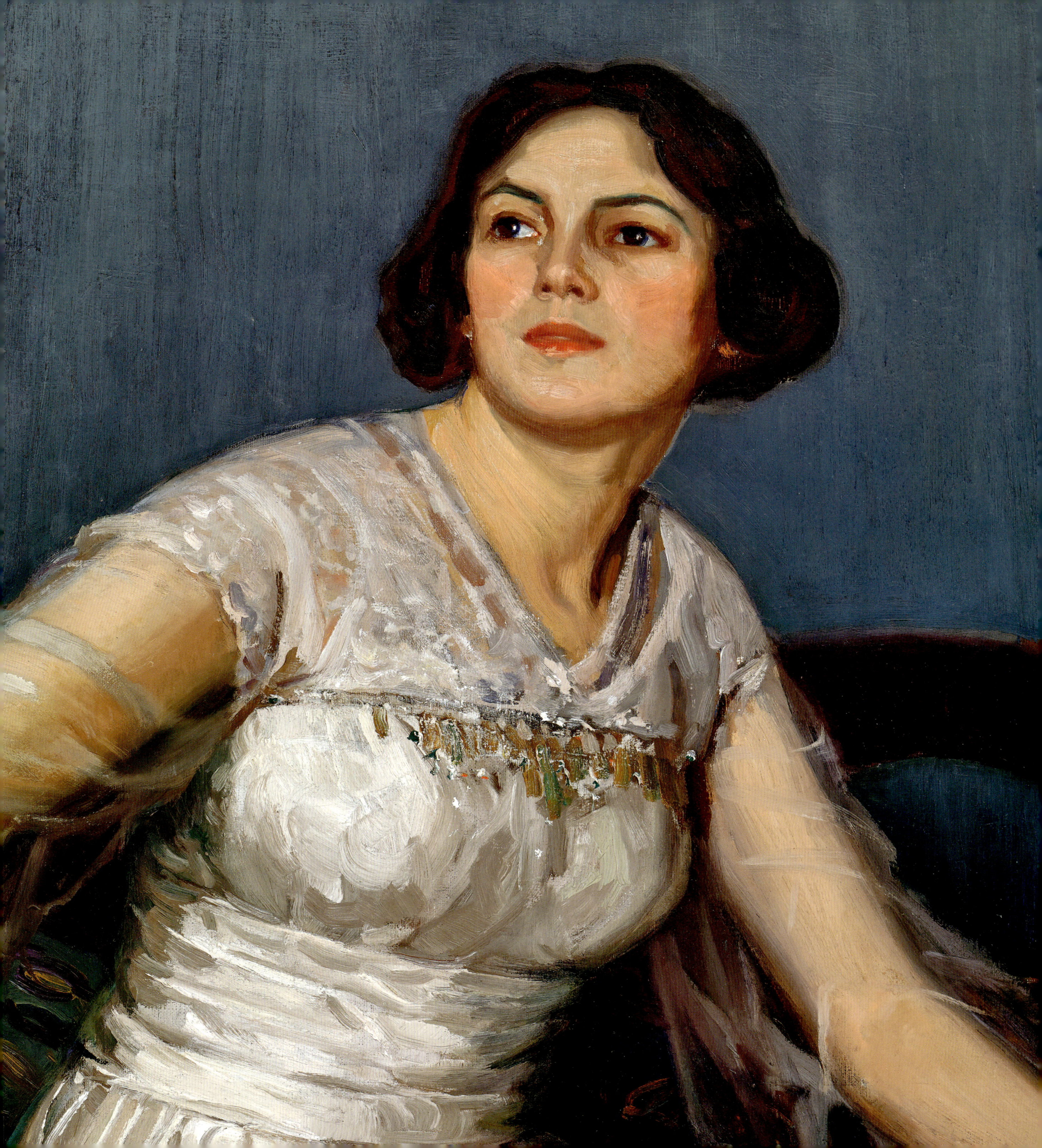

cheeks," with a "tinge of rose," and "the pearly and opalescent tones of the white satin gown," which made "a fine foil for the vivacious face with its frame of dusky hair." He noted that her curvaceous, shapely figure was revealed by the soft, flowing satin fabric of her dress, its butterfly sleeves of silk net edged with embroidered metallic thread, sequins, or crystal beads, all inspired by the Ballets Russes.

Costume and textile authority Edward Maeder has also elaborated on Edna's costume: "It seems that the figure is wearing a corset. The straight line of her back and the way she is seated on the settee look formal, even though the artist's casual placement of her right hand on the hip and her left hand carelessly draped over her left knee give the opposite impression. . . .There is an indication that the 'v' of the neck has been strengthened by the 'insertion' of a pink silk satin ribbon. This would, again, have been typical [of the period] and would emphasize the femininity of the sitter and show off her pale skin. The transition of style change is illustrated by the use of flimsy, nearly see-through textiles such as the light satin and the silk net that were a prelude to the outrageously 'indecorous' styles of the 1920s, when 'naughty' flappers let nearly everything show."

Maeder further believes that the sitter is wearing lipstick and rouge, which were acceptable for that period of time. The author feels that Edna's formal costume strongly suggests that she was a modern woman who stayed abreast of fashion and paid attention to her appearance.

MISS KETCHUM, c. 1918

Oil on canvas, 42 x 36 inches
Private Collection

AROUND 1918, KLEITSCH PAINTED a portrait of a young, attractive, independent woman, a successful New York designer who was visiting the Kleitsches in Chicago. An art critic later mentioned that "her direct personality [was] conveyed through her striking pose and her deep-set, gray-blue eyes" (*South Coast News*, October 10, 1930). Her individual expression and free thought are particularly discernible in this non-commissioned portrait, vividly evidenced by her determined face, her eyes, her expressive hands, and her shapely figure in costume. "Hats will be worn" was the order of the day in 1918, but in *Miss Ketchum*, the hat is not worn, but held. The small red tam in her right hand indicates a break from the established norm, but she still maintains some decorum, convincing the viewer that the hat is available, if needed. Edward Maeder has remarked that "her attire suggests a proper dress for a spirited walk through the woods for exercise. As a liberated woman, she is not wearing a corset, but she looks comfortably chic nonetheless. The stylish placement of the red sash, with its soft bow just in front of her right hip, was apparently arranged by the artist." He further stated that "her less-than-perfect hairstyle indicates that fashion is not everything to her, in character with her independent personality." This was a spontaneous portrait of a modern and trendy woman whom the artist knew very well as a close family friend.

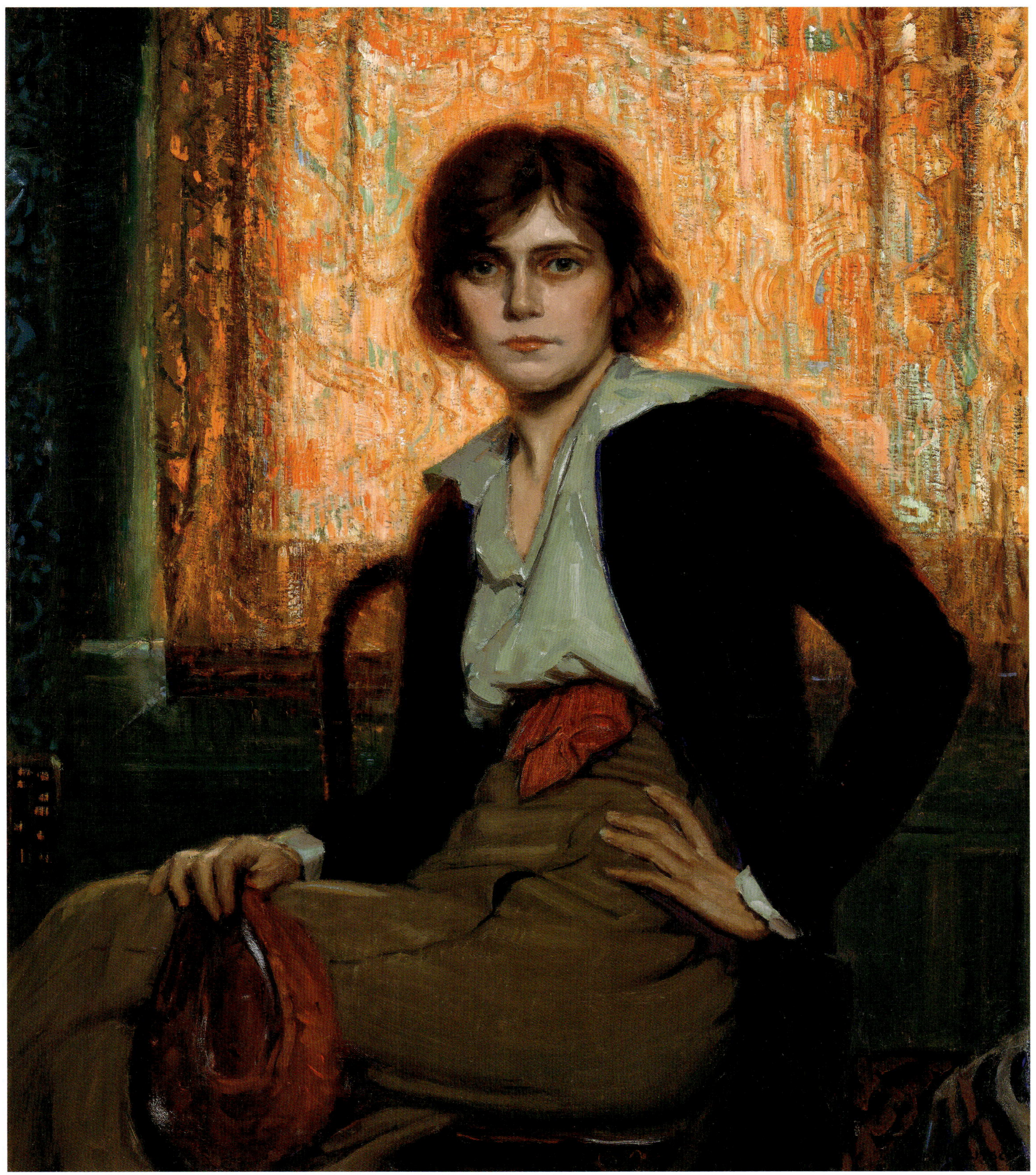

THE ATTIC PHILOSOPHER, 1916

Oil on canvas, 36 x 28 inches
Collection of Mr. and Mrs. Thomas B. Stiles II

AS WITH THE PRIOR PICTURE, the familiarity of the sitter's personality and mannerisms are aptly conveyed in this non-commissioned portrait of a Kleitsch friend. A reviewer described the portrait in glowing terms: "We have a masterpiece in portraiture. The whole character of the blond dilettante, a young Swedish friend of the artist in Chicago, is here—the dreamer, the musician, the philosopher, the sensualist, and the idealist. Kleitsch saw so much that his friend was reluctant to continue the poses, hence the picture was three months in the painting" (*Los Angeles Times*, June 17, 1923). The artist captured the Nordic appearance of his friend in a subtle characterization. The full lips and liquid blue eyes emphasize the sensuality of this young man, whose bohemian lifestyle was known to his friends. To complete the portrait of his friend's personality, the artist shows a strand of hair curled on the forehead, a cigar, and a jaunty neckpiece. The sweeping brushwork replicates the sitter's animated personality and reflects the popular painting style of the Chicago portraitist Wayman Adams (1883–1959).

In this portrayal, the artist has resorted to the traditional nineteenth-century practice of contrasting the male sitter's face and hands with the darkness of a black jacket. This tradition began in the Renaissance, as shown in Titian's *Man with a Glove* (c. 1520). When Kleitsch painted this portrait, he was keenly aware of the National Association of Portrait Painters exhibition then on at the Reinhardt Galleries in Chicago, where a number of Old Master male portraits were on view.

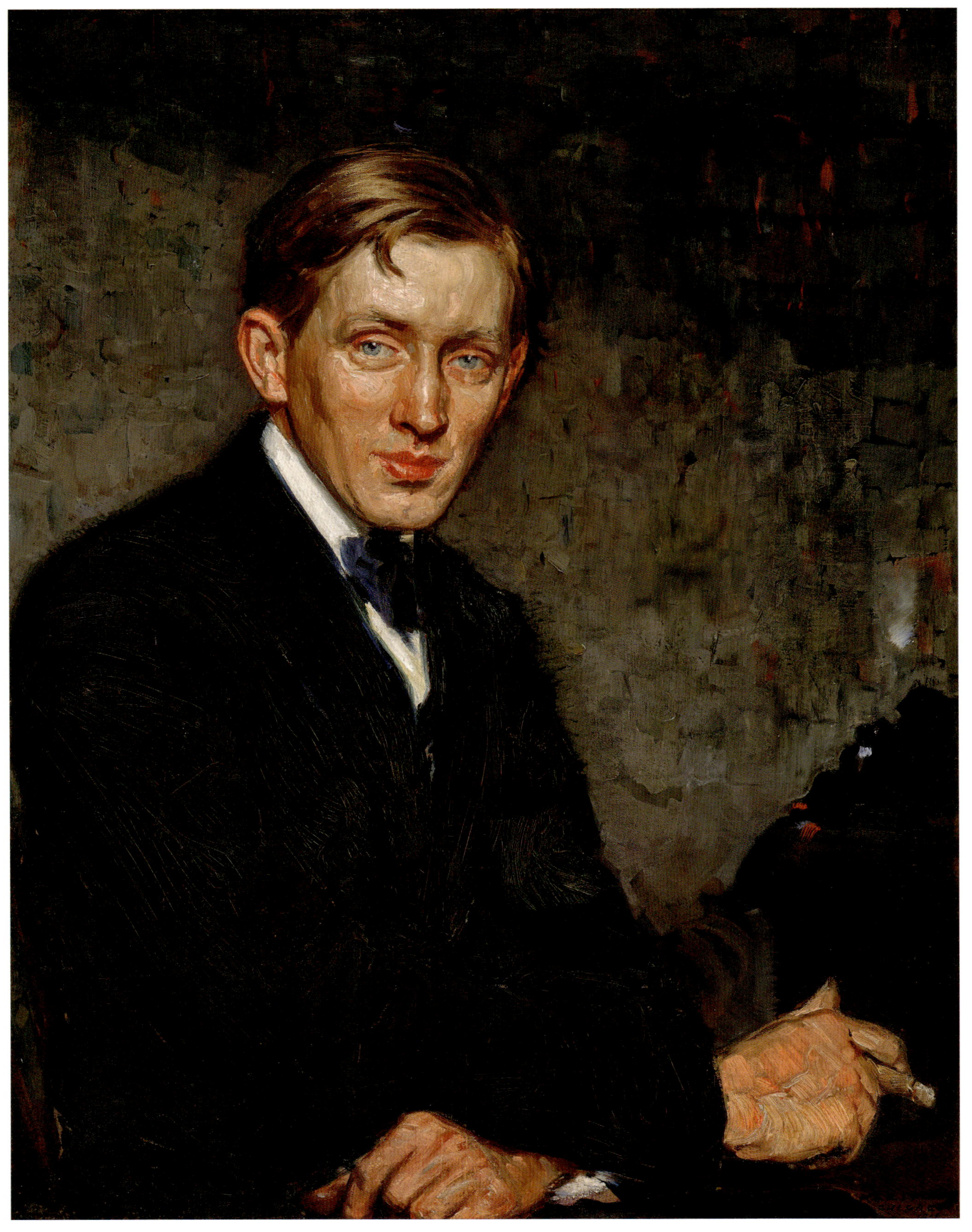

PROBLEMATICUS, 1918

Oil on canvas, 60 x 55 inches
Collection of Robert and Susan Ehrlich

WHEN *PROBLEMATICUS* WAS EXHIBITED at the Art Institute's Twenty-Second Annual Exhibition by Artists of Chicago and Vicinity in 1918, reviewer Lena McCauley singled it out as one of "the figure paintings to be remembered" (*Chicago Evening Post,* February 19, 1918). Enveloped in mellow luminosity, the figure seems lost in contemplation of a picture on the easel, most likely of herself. Perhaps she is puzzled by the artist's treatment of the subject, given the title assigned? Typical of several paintings of this period, Kleitsch has used backlighting that flows through the amber-colored window shade to create a mood and cast highlights on her body, recalling the influence of Vermeer and other Dutch artists. The close tonal values of gold and gray-blue give the work an elusive, poetic quality, and the colorful decorative patterning and contemporary design of the rug seem to recall the influence of Matisse. The textured gray-blue wall offsets the decorative patterning in the rug and creates a backdrop for the figure. Much later, in Kleitsch's California paintings, a cascade of color and decoration would become his hallmark.

Edward Maeder has written about the costume in *Problematicus*: "It appears to be a typical dress of the period, which probably has an over-panel of embroidery that falls from the shoulders, is held in place at the waist (both in front and back). The apparently transparent over-sleeves are typical of the period. One of the most interesting aspects is her hair. It is Greek in inspiration, with the swept-back look and the modified, almost 'bun-like' knot at the back. One finds it in photographs, graphics, advertisements…in fact, everywhere! The tip of her shoe that protrudes looks to be a similar color to the under-sleeves. The shoe is most likely satin but metalicized leather shoes were also popular at this time. It was a revival from the 1870s."

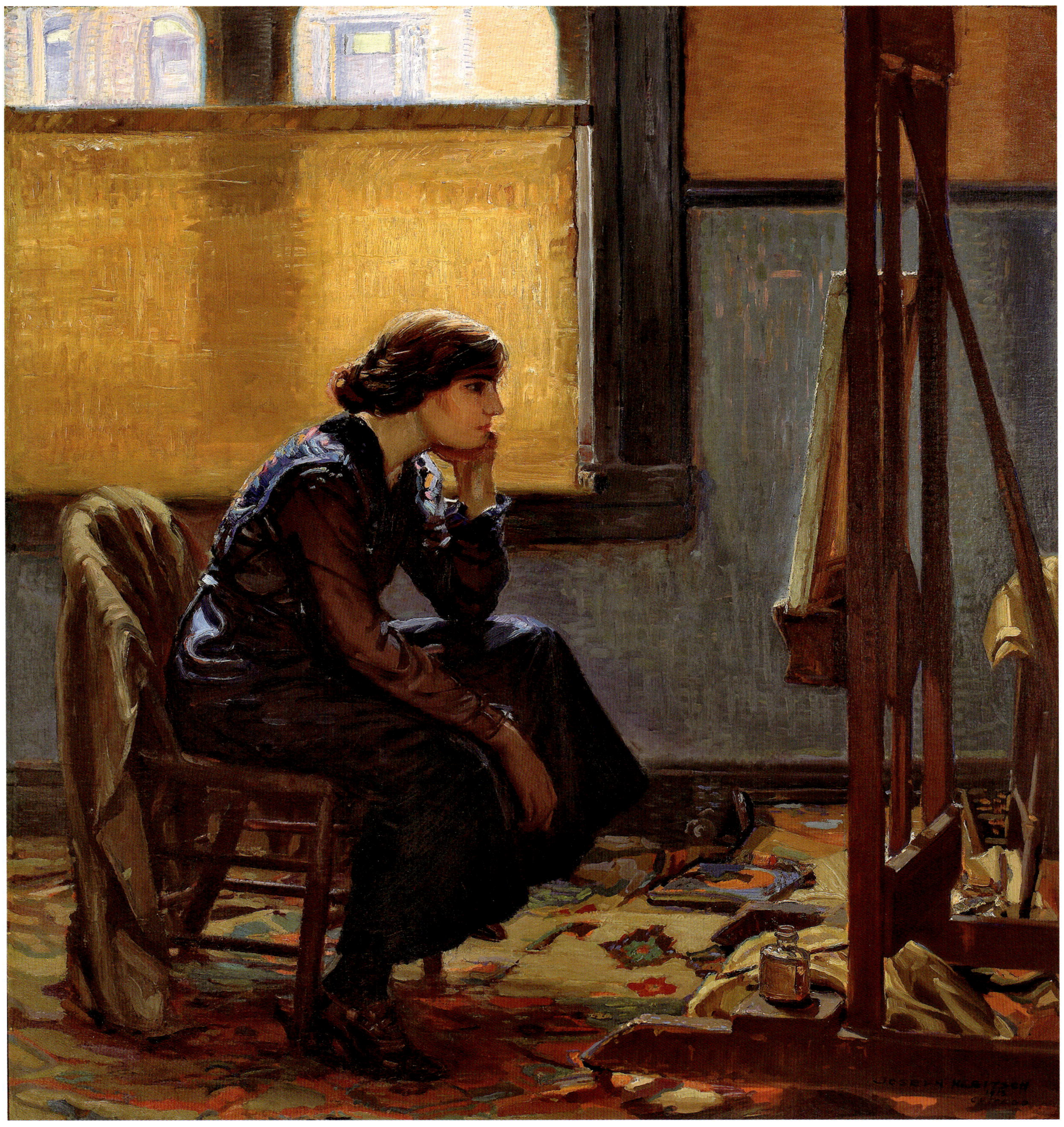

PORTRAIT OF ISADOR BERGER (RHAPSODY), 1917

Oil on canvas, 40 x 30 inches
Private Collection

IN 1917, KLEITSCH PAINTED a portrait of another close friend, a Chicago violinist who had composed the musical score for the artist's nonobjective painting *Chemistry*, shown in the Palette and Chisel Club's First Annual Abstract Art Exhibition. The painting, which was accidently destroyed, was described as "a wild conception of atoms, molecules and gases gyrating in prismatic form," and the violinist's composition was referred to as a symphony full of color and movement. Berger and Kleitsch had met in Chicago, where the musician was a soloist and concertmaster of the Chicago Philharmonic Orchestra as well as a violinist in the Chicago Civic Opera and Chicago NBC orchestras. Berger had received his doctorate from the Royal Conservatory in Brussels, where he had performed as first violinist in King Albert's Royal Court Orchestra.

Kleitsch's keen appreciation for music led him to support the orchestra, and he was befriended by several of its members. (He could very well have pursued a career in music himself, with his skill at playing the violin, flute, and accordion.) When he received the portrait commission from his friend, Kleitsch thought carefully about how to portray the musician. The finished painting captures Berger's musical virtuosity and suggests the beauty of the sound of a Stradivarius in the hands of an accomplished performer.

When Kleitsch exhibited Berger's portrait in the Annual Exhibition of the Palette and Chisel Club in April 1918, Evelyn Marie Stuart of the *Fine Arts Journal* commented: "Where have we seen more spirit or absorption in the theme than in Kleitsch's master interpretation of a well-known musician wrapped in his virtuosity? Is not this the very essence and spirit of the man it portrays and does it not suggest life, action, rhythm and all that one associates with a musician?" The artist has managed to capture the experience of a beautiful violin sonata and the intensity of its performer by sharply illuminating the sitter's face, hands, and flashing bow. In *Rhapsody*—Kleitsch's alternate title—the violinist is superbly posed and lost to the outer world in an ecstasy of musical interpretation. Berger was so deeply impressed by Kleitsch's portrait that he had it reproduced on the cover of a concert flyer.

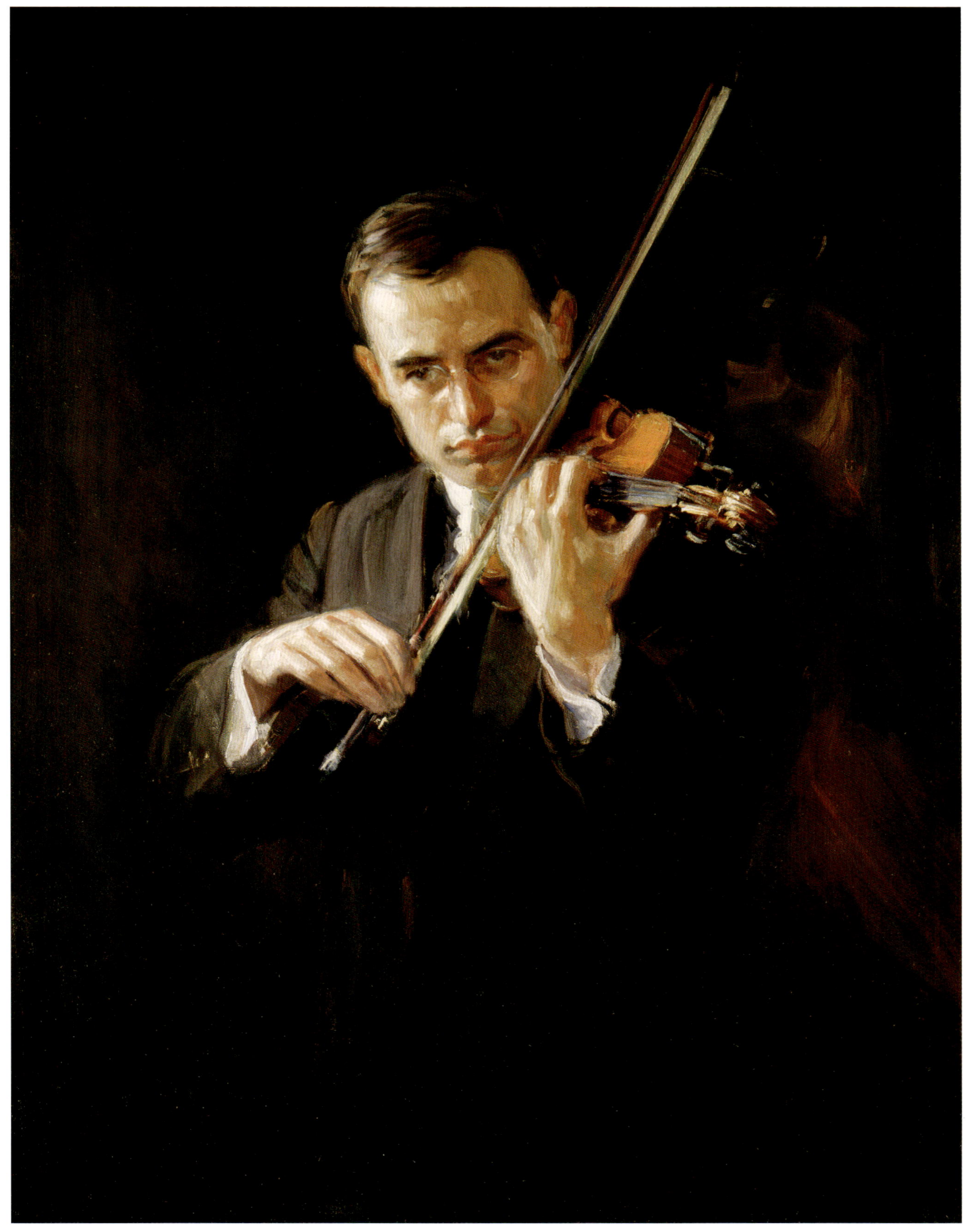

MISS GREGG, c. 1919

Oil on canvas, 48 x 30 inches
Collection of Michael Kizhner Fine Art

AS TEENAGERS, EDNA AND HER SISTER Martha were known as the "belles" of Grand Rapids, Michigan. Edna was reputed to have been born there on January 16, 1890, but her birthdate and birthplace are not documented by a Michigan birth certificate. According to the 1910 U.S. census, her mother did not arrive in America until 1892, two years after Edna's supposed birthdate. Researcher David O'Hoy checked the grave marker where Edna is buried and found the year of birth listed as "1888." Later, Janet Murphy, another researcher, obtained a copy of her Confirmation of Naturalization and U.S. Citizenship, documenting the fact that Edna was born in Lithuania in 1888. Nothing is known about Martha's birthdate and birthplace, or whether she was born before or after her sister; however, we can comfortably assume that she was also born in Lithuania.

It appears that the sisters spent their youths in Grand Rapids, where their parents worked in the booming furniture factories. In an interview with Michael Kelley, an art dealer in Los Angeles, Edna's godchild Marianne Barto said that Martha Gregaitis had lived in a convent for thirteen years as a member of a religious order; she then moved to Chicago, where she became a teacher in the public schools and later an officer in a truant school.

After Martha became established in Chicago, she made an effort to change her persona, choosing "Marcia" as her given name and "Gregg" as her surname. She and Edna closely resembled each other and were equally attractive, tall, and statuesque. To please his wife, Kleitsch painted a portrait of Marcia sitting in a chair, wearing a richly embroidered lavender silk blouse and a gold-colored shawl casually draped over her shoulders and arms, complementing the warm flesh tones of her smiling face, framed by her dark hair. Like her sister, Marcia was very conscious of the latest designs in women's wear. Marcia later married businessman A. Paul Jones in Chicago; when Edna was suddenly widowed in 1931, he supported her through severe financial difficulties.

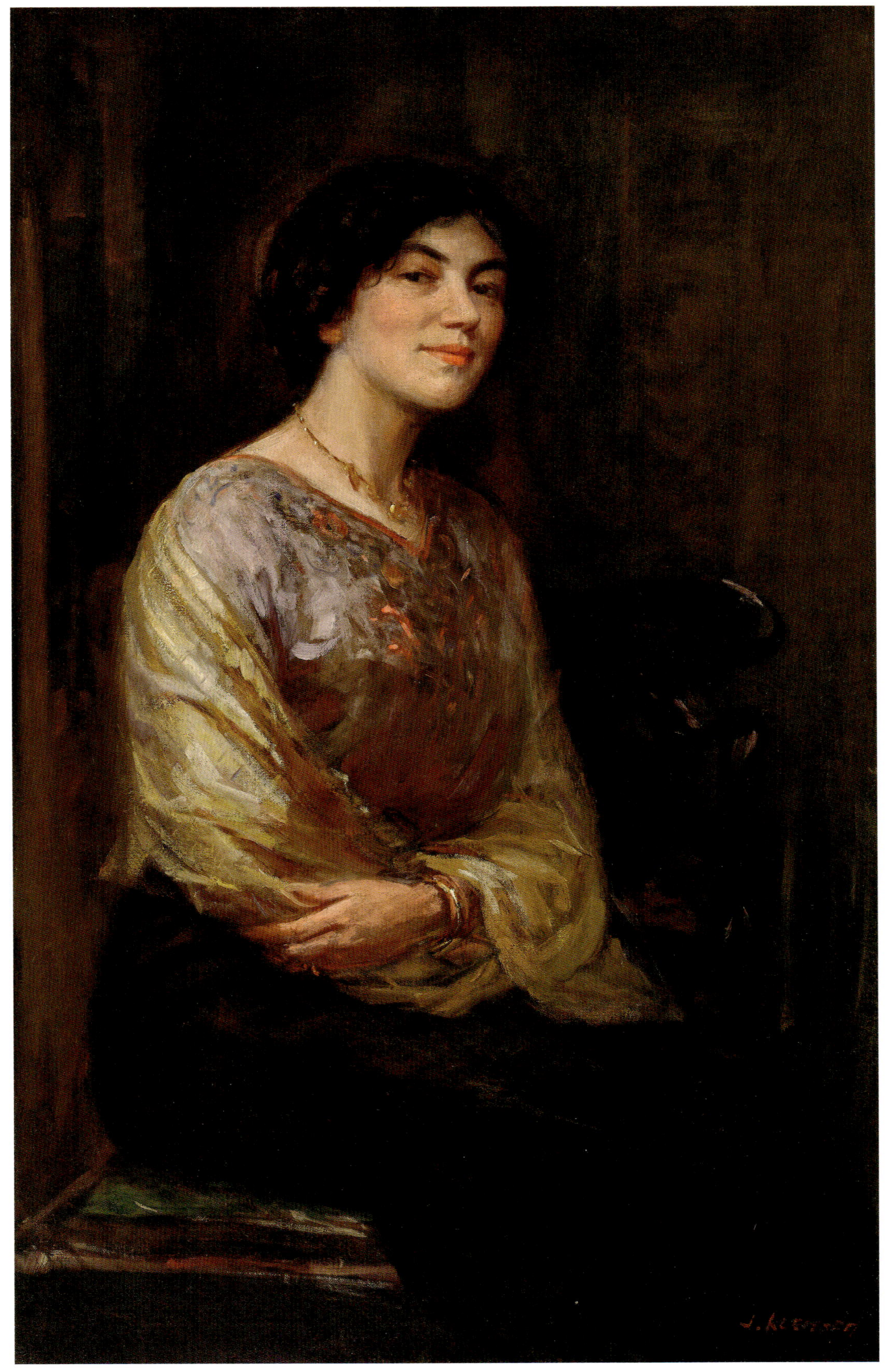

PORTRAIT OF DR. WALTER JARVIS BARLOW, c. 1921–22

Oil on canvas, 36 x 32 inches
Collection of Barlow Respiratory Hospital

BARLOW RESPIRATORY HOSPITAL traces its heritage to the dedication, passion, and vision of its founder, Dr. Walter Jarvis Barlow (1868–1937), who purchased acreage in the Chavez Ravine community of Elysian Park, near what is now Dodger Stadium, and built the Barlow Sanitarium in 1902. While still a young physician in New York, Barlow had faced his own challenge when he contracted tuberculosis and realized that there was a need for better diagnosis and treatment of this dreaded disease. In the sanitarium's rudimentary state—tents and cottages served as buildings—Dr. Barlow and his staff began treating patients for tuberculosis and eventually expanded into all respiratory ailments.

A well-respected figure in Southern California, Barlow served on a number of committees and was one of the area's leading social figures. As he was an art collector, it was natural that he would be selected to serve on the first art committee of the prestigious Los Angeles Athletic Club, which in 1912 occupied its recently built Beaux-Arts clubhouse, designed by John Parkinson. The committee's objective was to secure a representation of the best of Southern California art, in order to enhance the elegant new building.

It has been very difficult to identify the provenance of Kleitsch's portrait of Barlow. In fact, the painting was not even recognized as being by Kleitsch until the author's visit to the hospital several years ago. It likely was commissioned through the aegis of Earl Stendahl, who had appointed Kleitsch his portrait painter and had secured other commissions for him. Stendahl's records do not note such a portrait, according to his biographer April Dammann, but there was a close relationship between the Barlow and Stendahl families.

Here, Kleitsch's ability to fully capture the demeanor of this eminent doctor is enhanced by the painting's background, showing medical instruments and books of his profession. Although his dark suit was typical of his normal attire, the bright red tie and colorful ring would seem to indicate a flair for styling of the period.

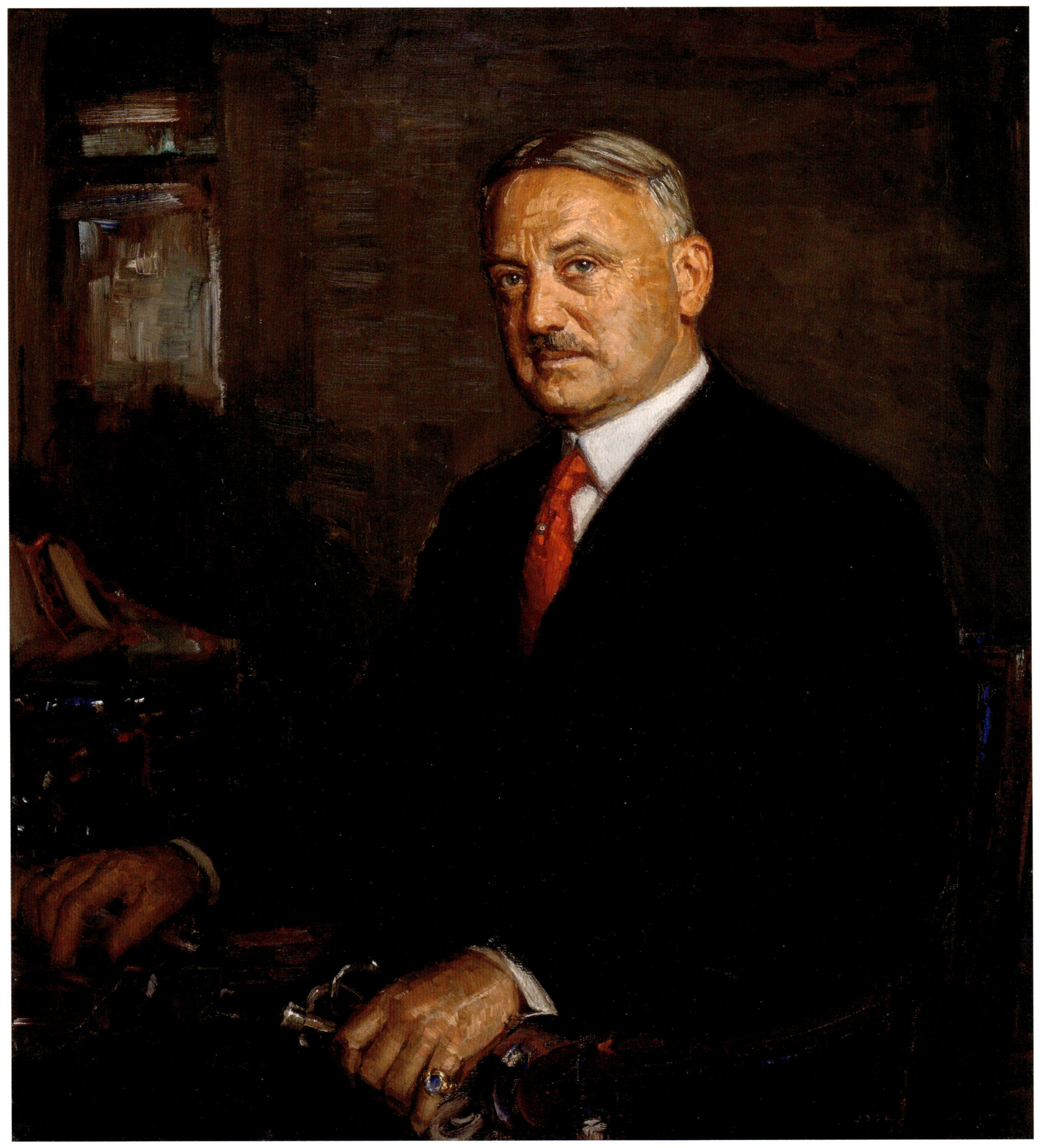

PORTRAIT OF ARTIST ROBERT FULLONTON, 1921

Oil on canvas, 40 x 34 inches
Laguna Art Museum Collection, Gift of Marjory Adams Darling

AMONG KLEITSCH'S LAGUNA FRIENDS, the artist Robert Fullonton (1876–1933) became a subject for his brush. Unlike the pictures of other male friends, Kleitsch chose to portray him in a semiformal dress and setting. The seriousness and candor of his friend's personality is the focus of this portrait. Fullonton's piercing blue eyes, seen through pince-nez, along with his patterned tie, provide focal points of color against the flesh tones and the neutral, textured background. The portrait is a dichotomy, portraying the sitter's relaxed yet alert demeanor.

Kleitsch's distinguished portrait of his well-educated and sophisticated friend belies the actual financial difficulties that Fullonton and his mother, also an artist, experienced in Laguna. Both mother and son, who lived together, were unable to sell their paintings, and ended up giving them away. He died in 1933, disappointed and destitute.

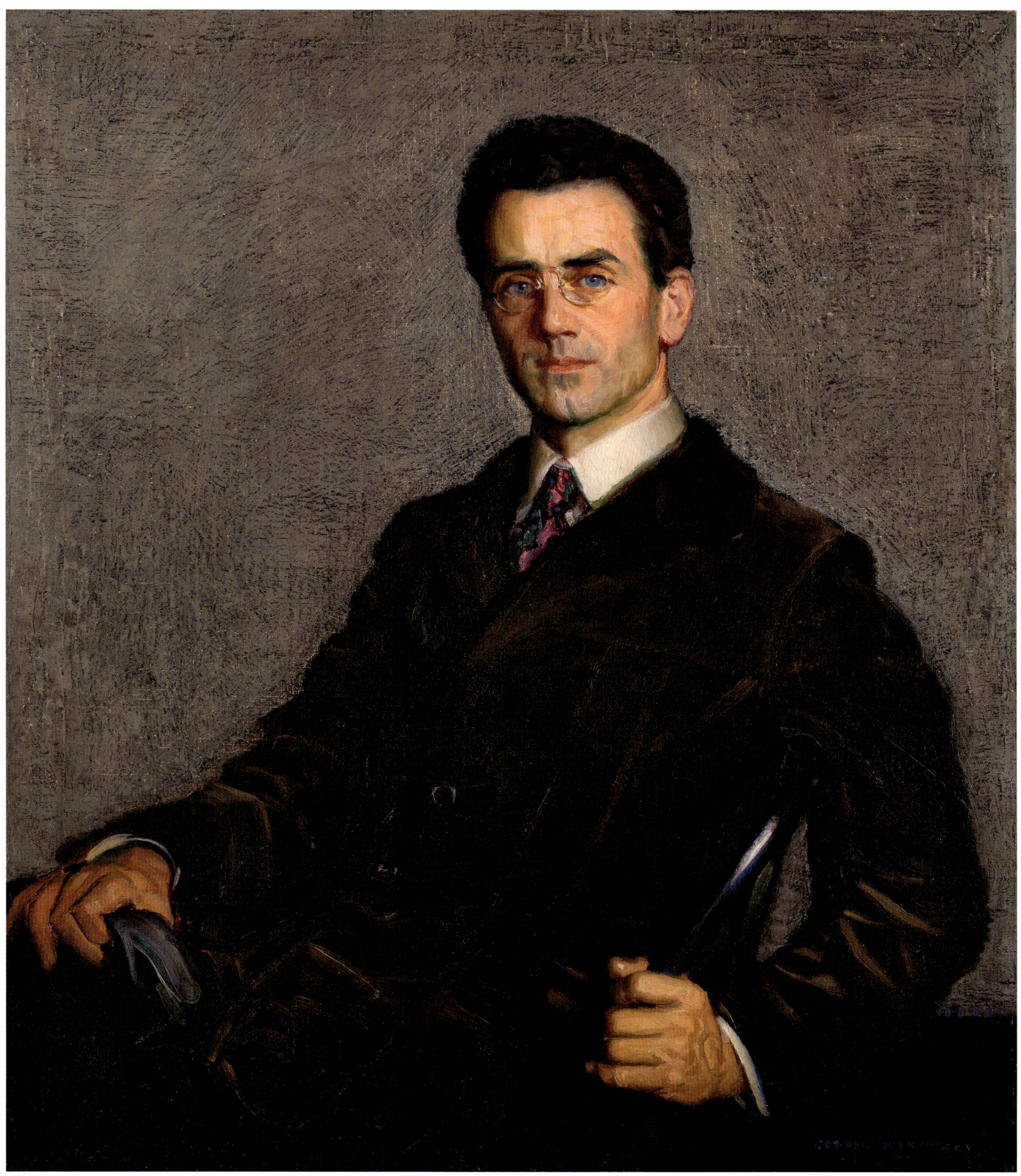

THE ORIENTAL SHOP, 1922

Oil on canvas, 32 x 40 inches
Crocker Art Museum, Melza and Ted Barr Collection

AS KLEITSCH BECAME MORE ESTABLISHED as a painter, his compositions began to display rich, vivid decorative patterns with chromatic effects. This typically rhapsodic expression can be observed in several of his California paintings, in which he seems to have fully embraced the spirit of his early years and the influence of Hungarian painting. The depth and sensitivity of his understanding of color was newly awakened, as evidenced in *The Oriental Shop*, which dazzles the eye with a galaxy of colors and a profusion of decorative objects. In this painting, Kleitsch employs the entire color spectrum, giving the painting the opulence of movie palaces of the 1910s and 1920s, as the artist's virtuosic brush moves freely in swirling arabesques.

One of the models for this genre scene is the fair-complexioned redhead, Florence Marsh, wife of the manager of G. T. Marsh and Company, an Asian import shop at the Ambassador Hotel. She reclines in a wicker chair while Kleitsch's wife Edna, the brunette, sits opposite her. They are surrounded by a profusion of antiques and decorative objects. Kleitsch has sculpted the hands and faces of his subjects with a variety of colors to produce delicate or somewhat swarthy flesh tones that are glowing and opalescent. The light of lamps and mirrors, blending in a chromatic crescendo, reflects the rich colors of their hair. The artist has employed a tilted perspective to draw the eye back to the impressionistic, light-filled windows, somewhat reminiscent of the Tiffany windows of the 1920s; these reveal figures passing by in the arcade.

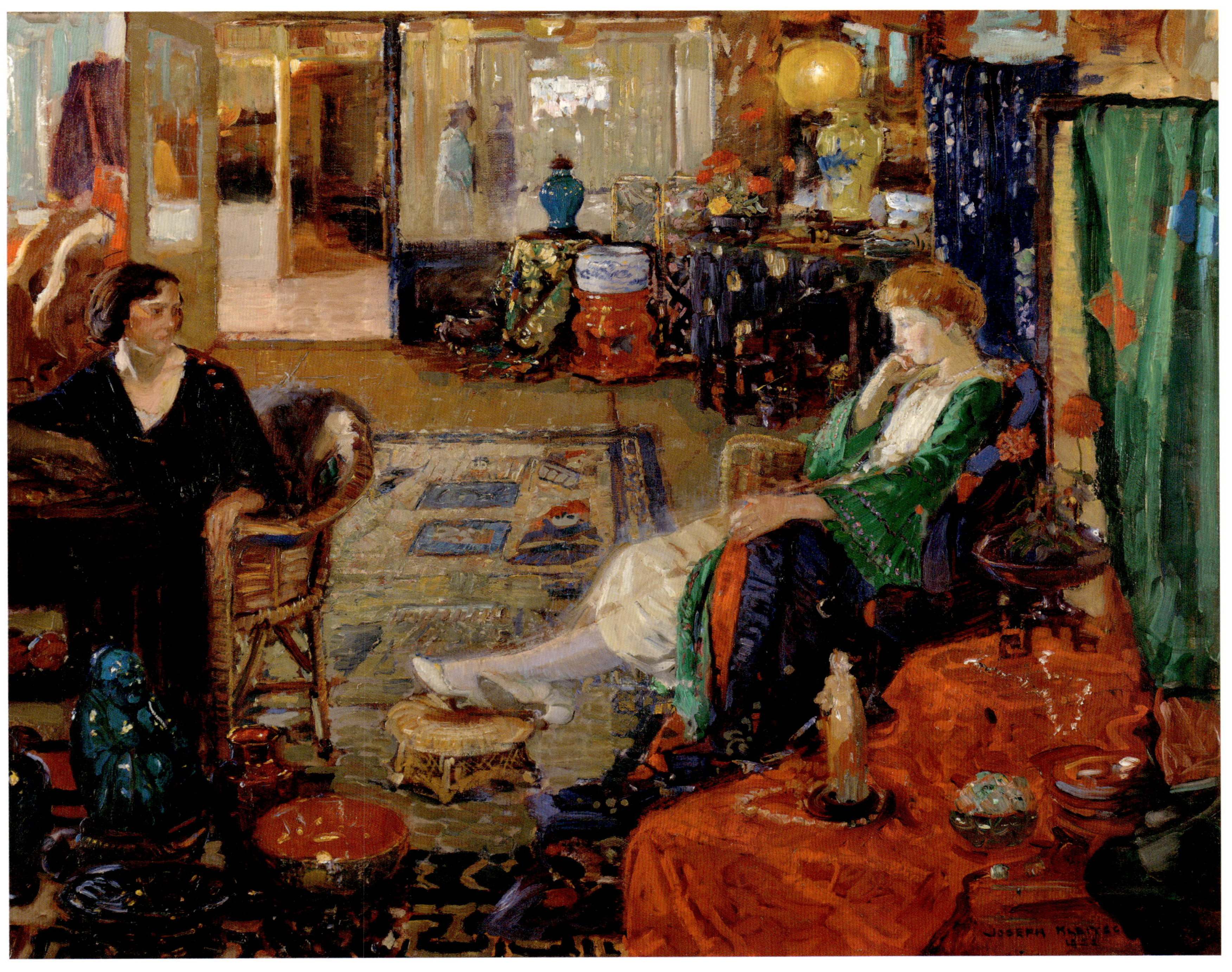
JOSEPH

THE ORIENTAL SHOP (THE JADE SHOP), 1925

Oil on canvas, 32 x 26 inches
The Irvine Museum

IN THIS SMALLER, ALTERED VERSION of *The Oriental Shop* (p. 65), the artist has included only a single figure, his wife Edna, who is almost incidental to the multicolored decoration and patterning. More abstract than the 1922 painting, this work appears to reflect a sudden change of mood and direction by the artist. In this picture, Kleitsch has resolved the final composition by reducing the painting's width to eliminate the profusion of folds of drapery shown strewn on the left side of the original version, evident in an early photograph.

In this later version, the artist has chosen the same location for his setting as in the 1922 version of *The Oriental Shop*—G. T. Marsh & Company, located on the arcade level of the Ambassador Hotel. Marsh's father, George Turner Marsh, had founded the House of Marsh in San Francisco in 1876, and he was one of the first to introduce Asian art to the West Coast. The company eventually had branches in Los Angeles, Santa Barbara, Coronado, and Monterey.

Many of the same Asian artifacts that grace the 1922 version can be seen here. In 1925, Kleitsch painted several vibrant and colorful scenes composed of these objets d'art for an exhibition at Stendahl-Hatfield Galleries. Art critic Antony Anderson exuberantly reviewed the show, writing: "Ah, those still-lives! You will pounce upon four or five in the gallery that are simply overwhelming in their virtuosity." Anderson continued to rhapsodize over the artist's ability to transform the canvas: "Kleitsch does make the canvas laugh for joy, and simply and solely because he himself is so joyful and expert, so absolutely alive, when he paints."

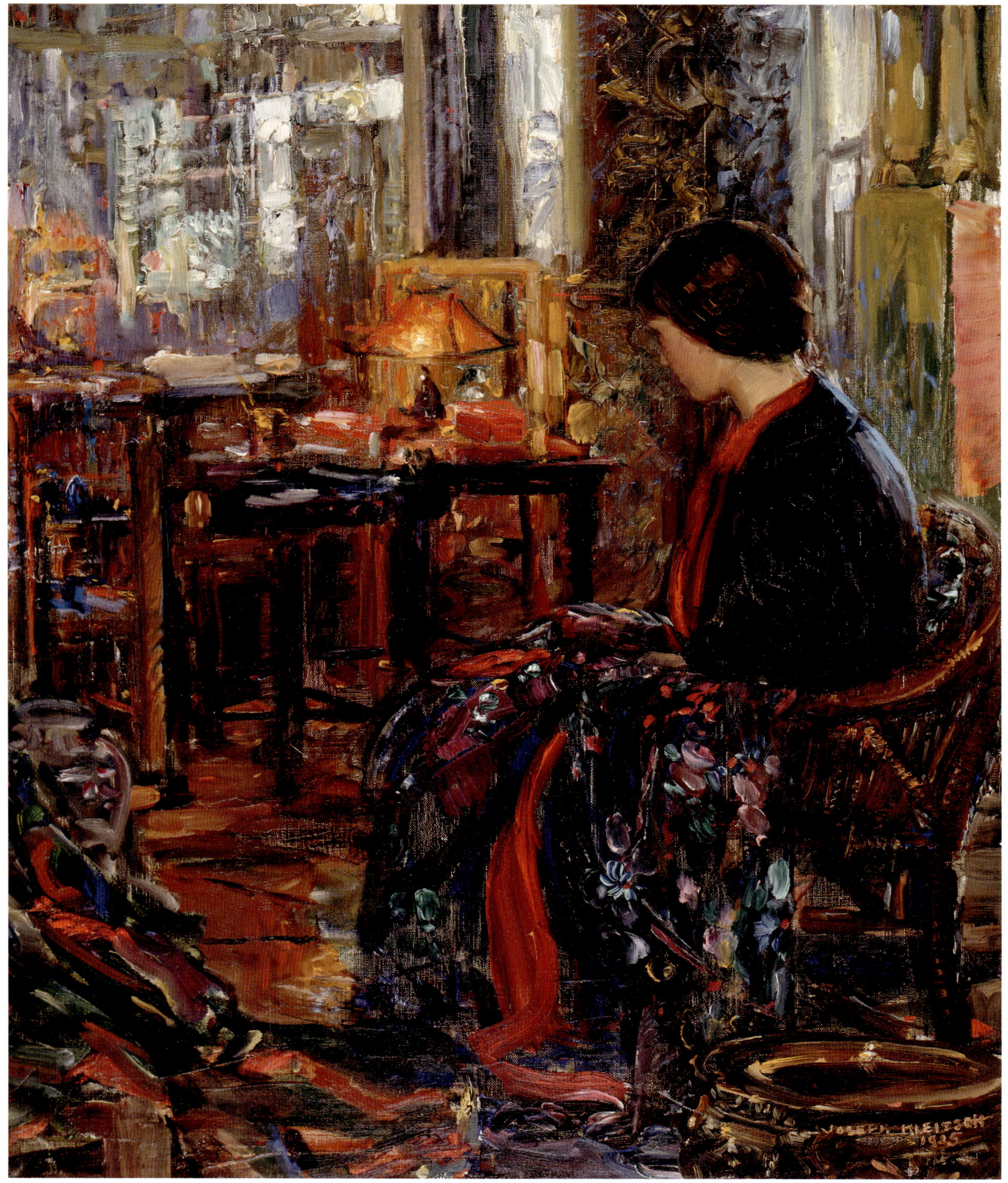

WILLIAM KLEITSCH, c. 1910–15

Oil on canvas, 40 x 30 inches
Private Collection

WILLIAM KLEITSCH, A COUSIN of the artist, is portrayed here as an attractive, sporty, self-confident individual. The painting itself reflects the physicality and strength of the sitter, who is posed as a successful businessman. The conservative suit—complete with a colorful, bold, patterned cravat and a starched, collared shirt—further reinforces his business-like demeanor, as painted by the artist, who knew him well. In addition, the cigarette in his right hand speaks to his masculinity. William was a member of the Kleitsch family who had settled in Cincinnati; it is probable that the artist painted his cousin's portrait when he took his first wife, Emma, to reside there with her family just prior to his move to Mexico in 1911. William later worked in Chicago, so the portrait could have been painted there instead, as he looks much older here than he does in a 1910 photograph, taken in Cincinnati with the artist and their cousins by marriage, Joseph and Philip Vollmer. The inscription of their names on the back of that photograph assisted with the identification of this previously unknown male portrait.

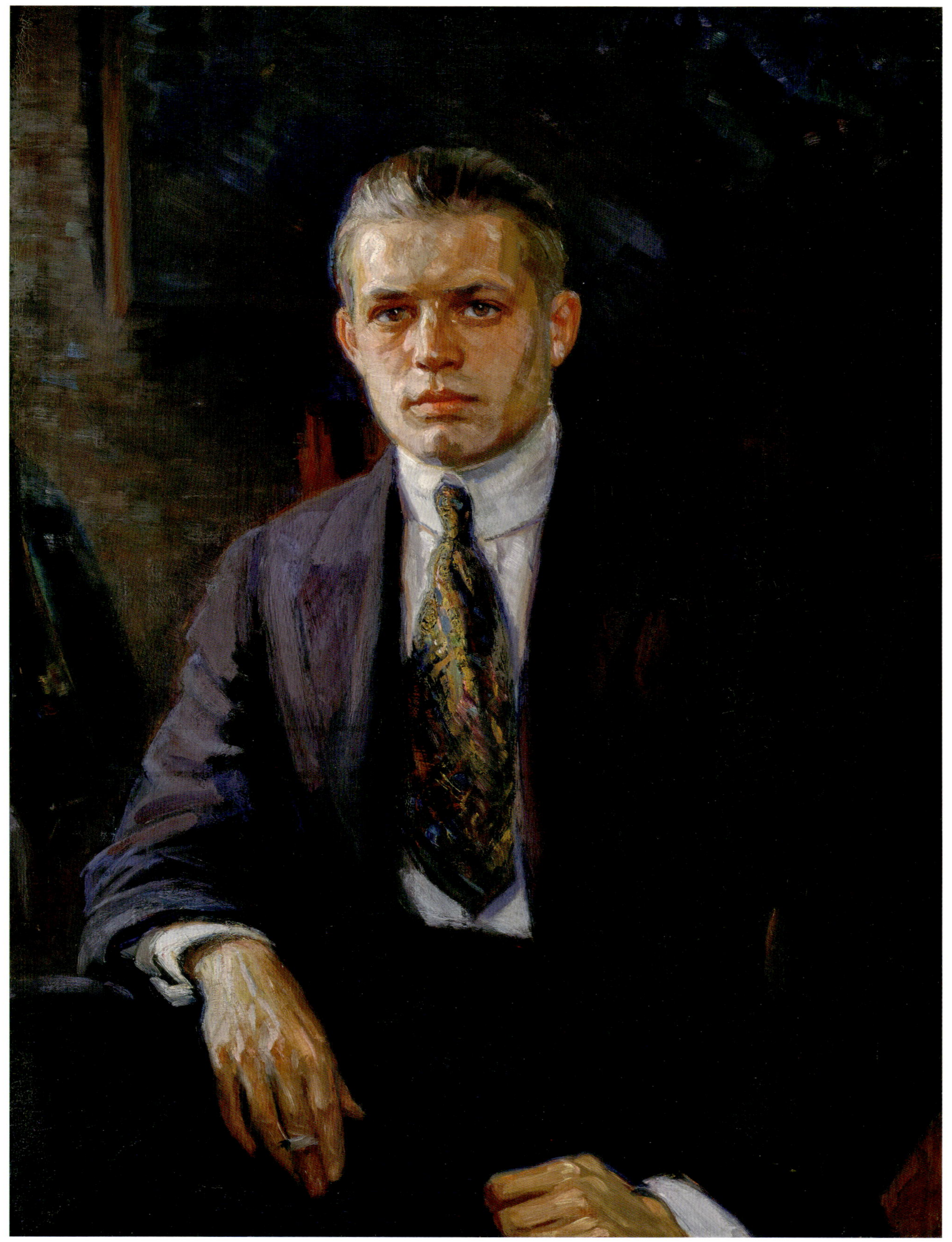

BEHIND THE FENCE, c. 1910–11

Oil on canvas, 38 x 24 inches
Courtesy of The Redfern Gallery

THE ARTIST AND HIS FIRST WIFE, Emma, left Mexico City in 1909 and moved to Chicago, where Kleitsch had relatives who could provide a supportive base for the couple. The primary motive for this move was the city's active art center with its large ethnic population, providing a favorable environment for a foreign-born person. Kleitsch, who was then an active practicing artist, was listed as a "resident-artist" in the census of 1910. Before his second visit to Mexico City in 1911, Kleitsch painted *Behind the Fence,* a realistic scene of two urchins hiding in an alley to steal a smoke. The subject recalls the many paintings of children and urchins by the American genre painter John George Brown (1831–1913), whose work Kleitsch undoubtedly knew from book illustrations. Based on a large number of photographs of underprivileged children, particularly of young boys who worked in the mills and factories, the painting can be dated to 1910–11. These "denizens of the alleys" typically wore short pants or knickers, long stockings, boots, and straw hats or caps. Shortly after Kleitsch completed the painting, the couple left for Cincinnati; due to Emma's frail health, she remained there with her family during the artist's second trip to Mexico City, in 1911–12.

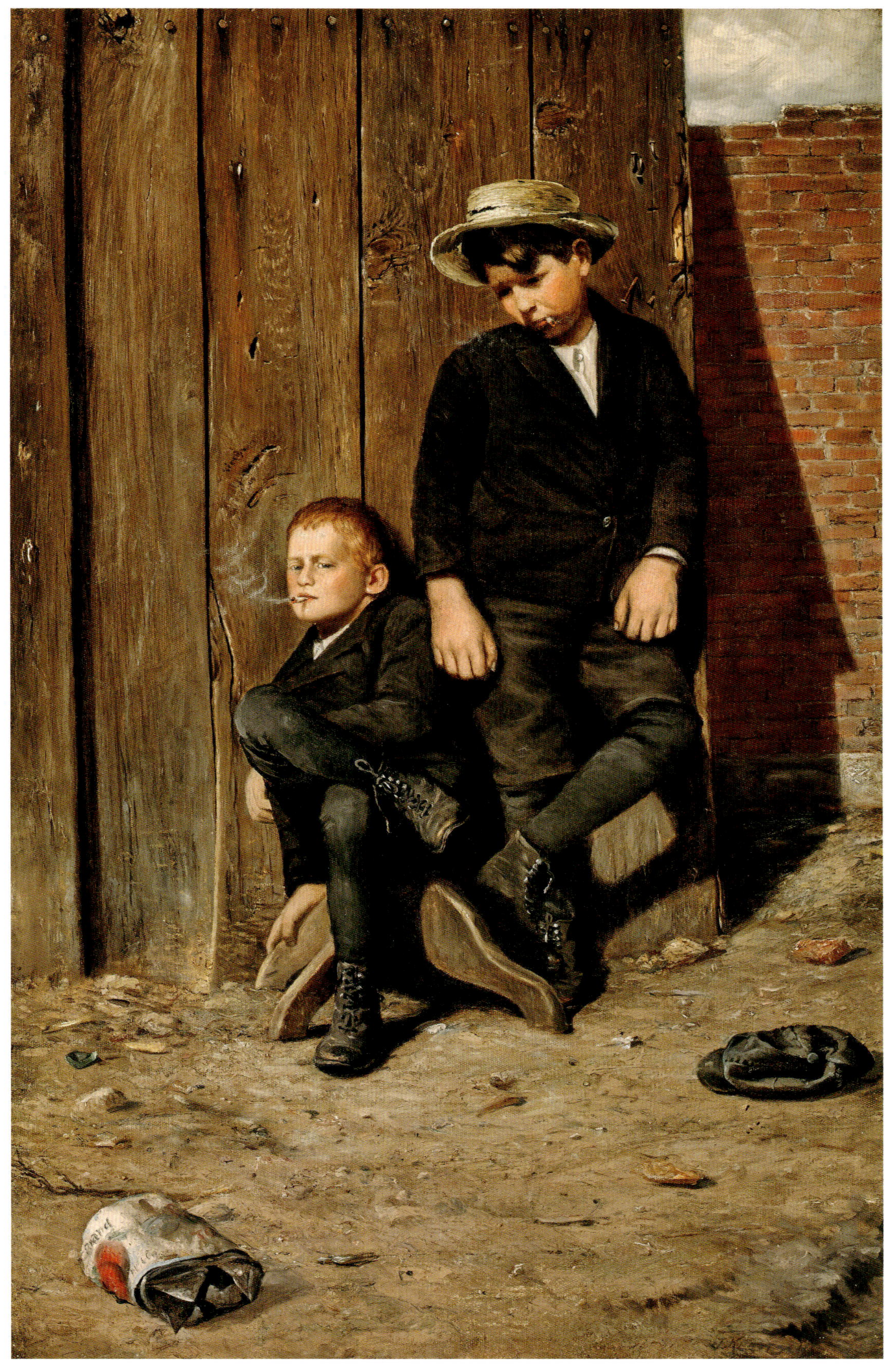

STUDIO INTERIOR, 1915

Oil on canvas, 30 x 40 inches
Collection of Simon K. Chiu

IN 1915, KLEITSCH LEASED a larger studio in the Athenaeum Building in Chicago and began to produce a variety of paintings. This space offered him a means of controlling the light and of increasing his exposure to other artists, primarily members of the Palette and Chisel Club. At this time, he began to experiment with interior genre scenes, expanding his creative talents. The studio, furnished with antique rugs and furniture, became the setting for many of his figure paintings. One of them, *Studio Interior,* captured the attention of a reviewer of the Palette and Chisel Annual Exhibition in April 1918: "No one, we venture to say, has ever offered a nude and steam radiators in the same room each as just an object in the scheme, the one not played up as a central figure, the other not appearing as an obtrusive novelty. Artists like this picture immensely because it shows the happy faculty of an artist in finding beauty in the commonest things. They delight in the fine bits of color afforded by the old rag carpet, cheap draperies and shabby studio properties—color which is just as clear and just as interesting as that of silks and velvets. The nude model seen through the dressing room door in the far corner is only an incident of the scene. A touch of winter outside the window adds to the effectiveness though it does not seem consciously introduced" (Evelyn Marie Stuart, *Fine Arts Journal*, April 1918).

Although the painting is primarily tonal, with close values, the artist's unusual dark colors appear to have become brighter. The painting offers a window into the artist's working space, displaying a casual assemblage of drapery and clothing, along with a diverse array of objects. A voyeuristic glimpse at an out-of-scale nude model dressing inside an open armoire recalls Degas's pictures of bathing women. In the adjoining room, the artist's easel is set up; light streaming through the window illuminates the studio and creates a subtle play of brightness and shadow.

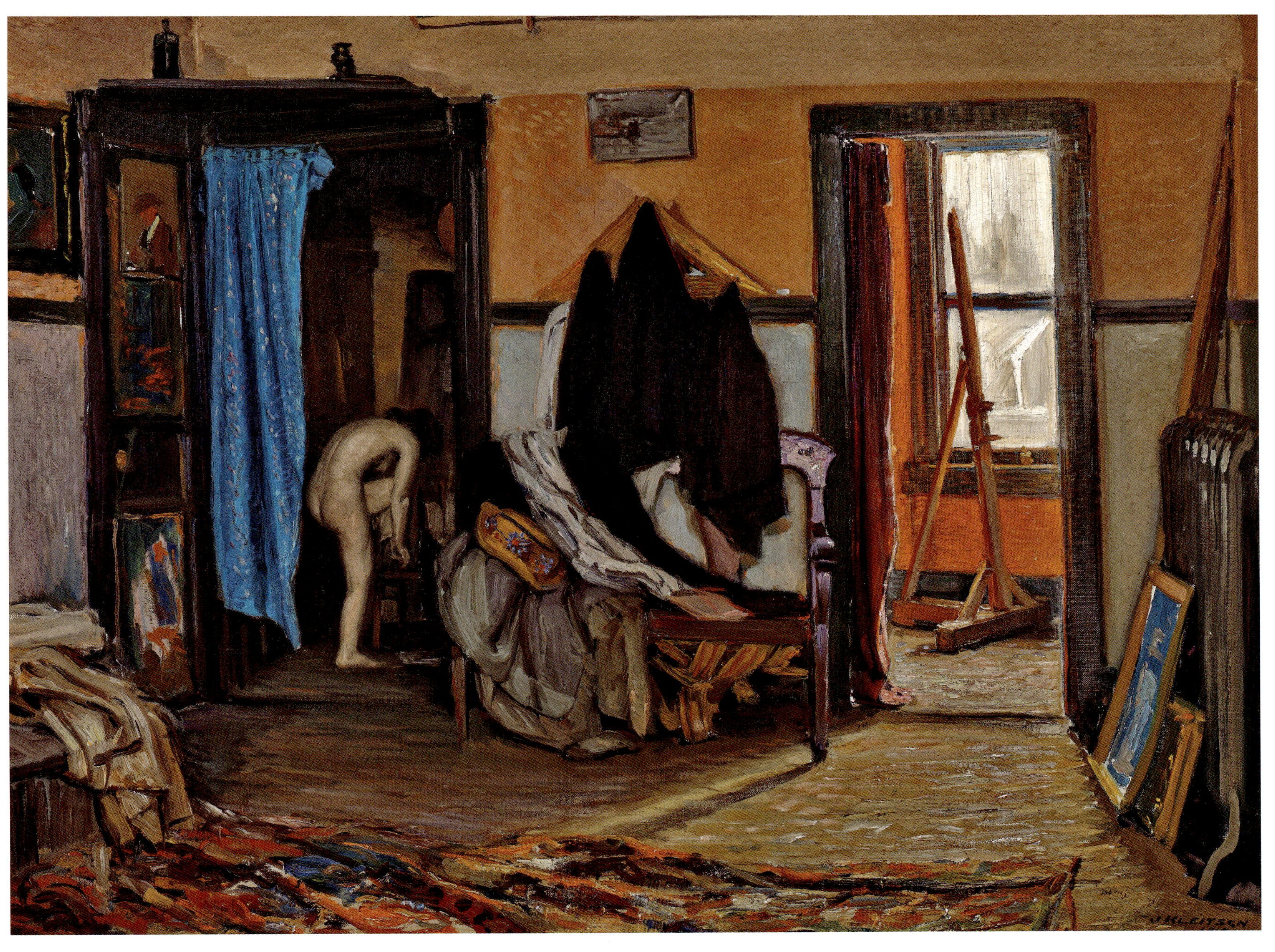

UNTITLED PORTRAIT IN ATHENAEUM CLUB ROOM, c. 1915

Oil on canvas, 33 x 25 inches
Collection of James Taylor and Gary Conway

IN ONE OF THE MORE ELABORATELY furnished Athenaeum club rooms, Kleitsch painted a figural interior scene with an unidentified woman seated in a chair, amongst antique furniture, decorative objects, and a beautiful rug. There has been speculation that the sitter is Miss Irene Petrtyl, the niece of August Petrtyl, president of the club in 1906, or a relative of Edna's from Lithuania, then part of Russia. However, August Petrtyl ruled out the possibility that his niece was the model for this picture.

Textile authority Edward Maeder has judged from the model's dress and hairstyle, and from her Russian appearance, that she could possibly be a relative of Edna's: "What looks like a fur hat is actually a voluminous hairdo, held with a hairband and layers of silk milliners' net over a buckram base. Parted in the center, the hair is combed rather close to the head, dips down over the ears and is then caught up in a bun at the back." Both the costume and hairstyle confirm the 1915 date for the painting. During the period following World War I, said Maeder, "women did not have exposed foreheads." Also substantiating the date for the painting is "the very full skirt with its wide flounce and natural waistline. (After 1917, women wore barrel skirts.) An overskirt flares to just below the knees, covering a longer skirt, which was quite full, probably gored and may even have a deep flounce along the lower edge." The traditional furnishings and accessories complement the woman's rich silk crepe-de-chine dress. The sitter's formal attire and fine jewelry do suggest that she is dressed for a very special occasion. Tribal rugs from the Caucasus and a Navajo blanket thrown over the piano round out the setting and add further exoticism to the scene.

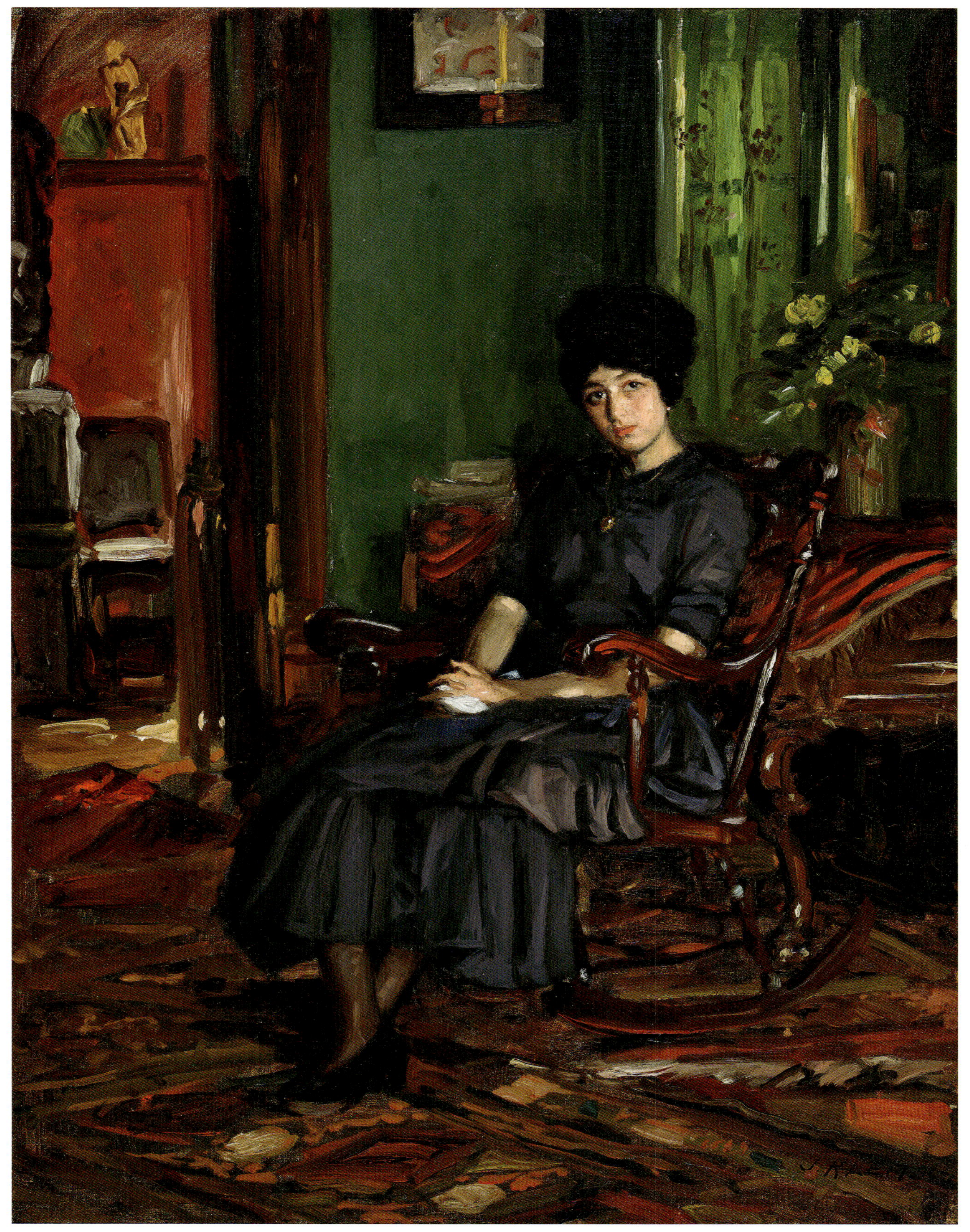

UNTITLED, 1911

Oil on canvas, 46 x 34 inches
Private Collection, from the Estate of Pearl Martin

WITH THE STIRRINGS OF the Mexican Revolution, which began in 1910, the volatile nature of Mexican politics made Kleitsch's visit to Mexico not only unsettling but also dangerous. The armed struggle between the diverse political factions of the population eventually forced President Díaz to resign. Despite the political chaos and uncertainty, Kleitsch found that living at the YMCA in Mexico City was very inexpensive, and this enabled him to continue his artistic career. In 1911 he painted a young Mexican woman swathed in colorful garments who, he said, reminded him of a childhood gypsy friend from his drawing class in Hungary. The nearly full-length figure is painted in an academic-realistic style of dark, neutral colors and posed in a rather stiff and conventional manner. The picture's veiled background, with its sketchy, colored images of a bed and a chair, suggest an intimate relationship between Kleitsch and the woman. Later in his career, rumors hinted of several affairs with women, which prompted certain members of his family to portray him as a "rogue."

When the artist exhibited the painting in June 1923, he related its background story to art critic Antony Anderson, who wrote: "It embodies an ideal held by the artist since his early childhood when he was a small boy in Hungary he and a little gypsy girl were the prize pupils in drawing, and he rather thinks the gypsy was ahead of him. She belonged to a tribe who were permitted to remain in the neighborhood because they were so peaceful and law-abiding. Joseph moved away, and when years later he saw a handsome Mexican girl of twenty-five in Mexico City, she seemed to be the very girl he had known so long ago—and so he painted her" (*Los Angeles Times*, June 17, 1923). (Today, Kleitsch's native city of Német Szent Mihály, a village in the Banat region of southwestern Romania, is occupied by gypsy families.) Kleitsch and Earl Stendahl listed the painting in a 1923 exhibition catalogue as "Gypsy." By the time of its purchase at the 1953 Edna Kleitsch estate sale, however, it had lost its title identification.

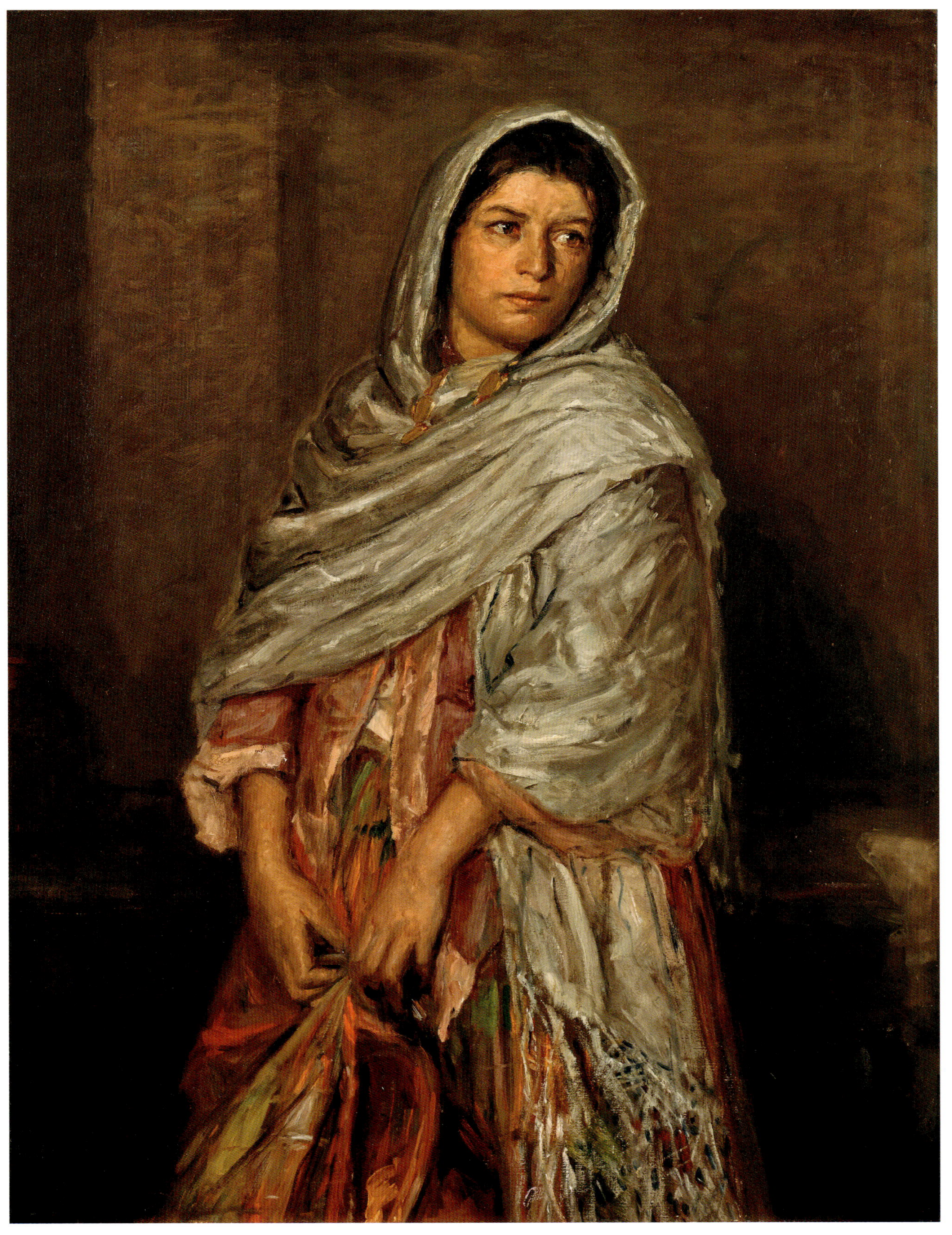

PORTRAIT OF RUTH RENICK (JADE NECKLACE), 1928

Oil on canvas, 35 ½ x 39 inches
Collection of Larane Rodnick

AFTER KLEITSCH RETURNED from an extended trip to Europe, as noted in the introductory essay, his commissioned portraits—such as those of Ruth Renick, Mrs. Marian Gould, and Ruth E. Bach—were painted in a highly mannered, theatrical style. The influences of French and English formal portraiture had not escaped his attention, and the attitudes of these models were influential in his later portraits. Fred Hogue's newspaper critique of Kleitsch's 1928 exhibition at the Stendahl Galleries included a reproduction of the portrait of the glamorous silent-movie actress Ruth Renick (1890–1984). This was not the original version of the painting, as it had been frequently altered as directed. Renick, who was born in Texas, was a prominent actress who had appeared in a number of early films, among them *The Mollycoddle* (1920), *The Witching Hour* (1921), and *The Fire Bride* (1922). In the present version of the painting, the sitter's pose has been varied slightly, with a jade necklace added to the final picture, and it is retitled *Jade Necklace.* This final version shows her almost subsumed in a highly decorative Hollywood interior setting. She wears a jacket with an Art Deco design of colorful flowers and ribbons over a white ruffled dress, and she sits at ease in an Aubusson chair in a theatrical and languid manner. The contents of the letter she holds are open to speculation. The artist has created a rough-textured, neutral background to offset the vibrant colors of her jacket and the smooth flesh tones of her face, which is highly rouged, with red lipstick. Her reddish-hued hair is loosely combed to her shoulders, in a style much in vogue in the 1920s.

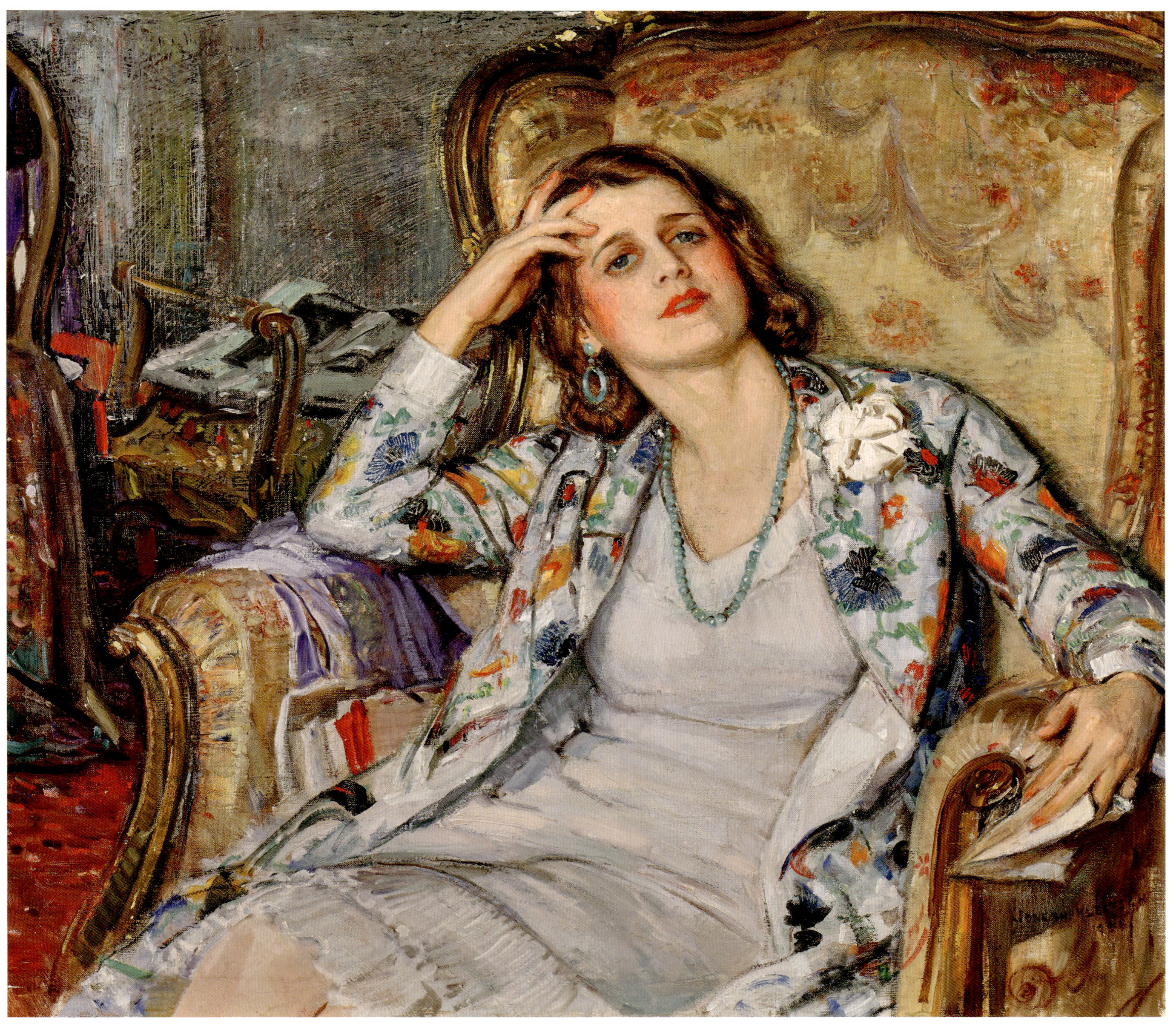

PORTRAIT OF MILDRED LAWRENCE, 1922

Oil on canvas, 24 x 22 ½ inches
Courtesy of George Stern Fine Arts

THE STENDAHL GALLERIES' HOSTESS, Mildred Lawrence, a favorite with the dealer's many patrons, also found herself a subject for the artist's brush. She had "tact, charm, unlimited patience, and moreover she was very good looking," as Kleitsch's fine portrait of her proves, and somewhat illustrates his seductive powers over some women. In this portrait from 1922, Lawrence sports the popular Roaring Twenties hairstyle of finger waves, and she is wearing glass beads, the fashion of the day. She wears a cover-up so that her dress will not get wrinkled or stained during the messy process of executing the finger waves with gel and water. Lawrence was an example of the perfect flapper. Her assured pose reflects a time of great change for women, with the right to vote finally at hand. In 1929, she left the gallery after her marriage to Allen Green, "leaving the patrons inconsolable" (Antony Anderson, *South Coast News*, January 25, 1929).

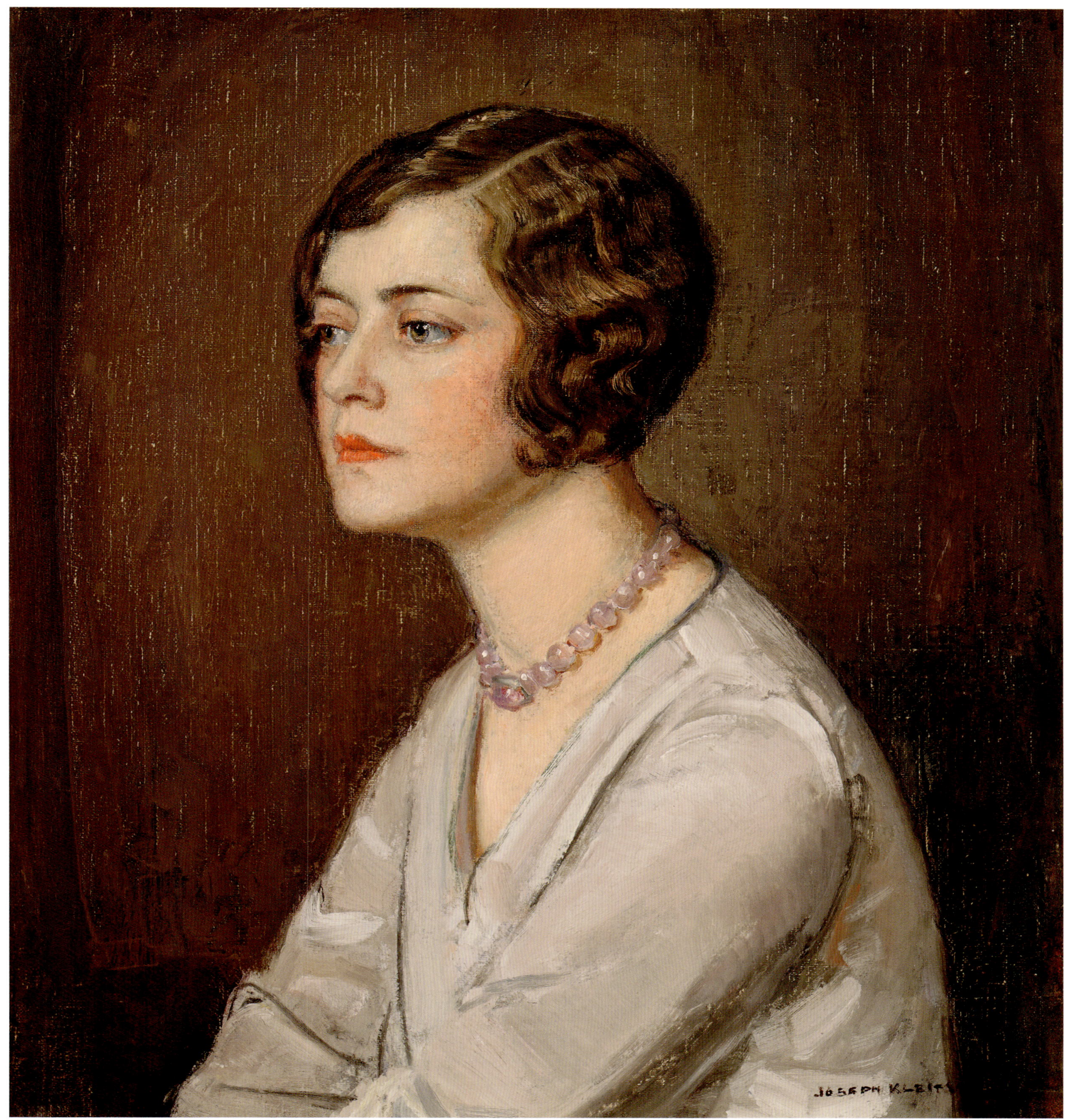
JOSEPH

Café las Ondas, c. 1930

Oil on canvas, 32 x 39 ½ inches
Private Collection, from the Estate of Pearl Martin

ONE OF KLEITSCH'S MOST captivating and ambitious compositions, with a complex choreography of figures parading and mingling up and down along Laguna Avenue, is *Café las Ondas*. In the 1880s, the café was a favorite gathering place for Laguna residents; it was then situated across from the Old Hotel Laguna's dining room. The café later became Dante's Nightclub and continued to operate until the 1970s, when the old buildings on Main Beach were razed to construct Main Beach Park. To capture a slice of everyday life in the beach city, the artist situated himself on the old boardwalk, looking up Laguna Avenue. The shaded blue structure with blue trim and arched windows on the viewer's left is the café; at its end are two figures at the crossing of El Paseo (the alley between the buildings fronting on the old boardwalk). Old Coast Boulevard crosses the avenue in front of the three tall eucalyptus trees. Kleitsch has cleverly chosen his view to juxtapose the bright California light and shadows of a late afternoon with ensembles of figures in various attitudes and activities. The costumes of the beach goers are colorful and varied, and these abstracted, gestural figures provide movement and visual tension. Kleitsch continued his experiment with abstract strategies but retained solid forms and naturalistic colors. The complexity of *Café las Ondas* sets it apart from the work of most other California plein-air painters of the era, as it requires time for the viewer to absorb the variety of activities that the artist had woven into his picture.

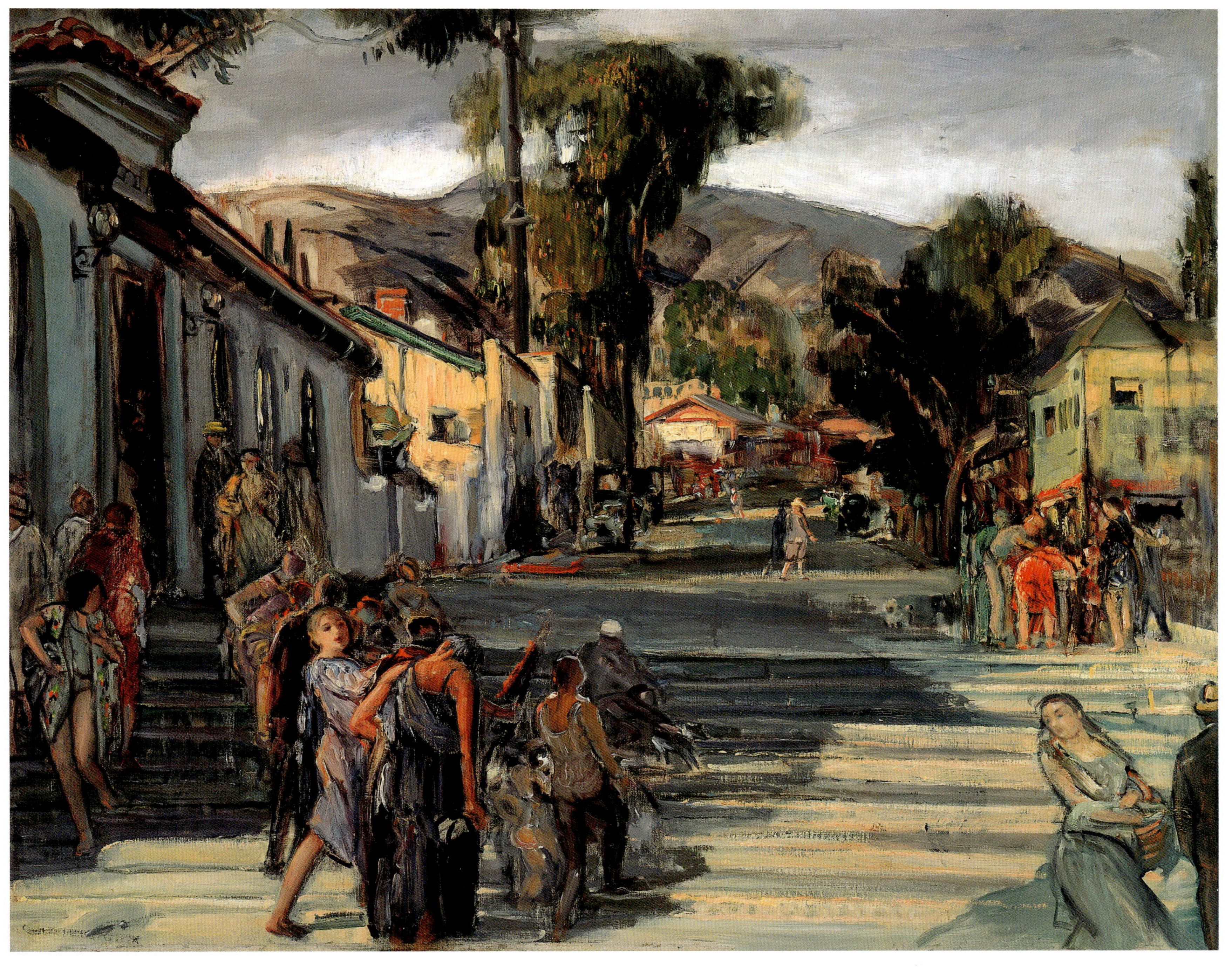

LAGUNA AVENUE AND HOTEL LAGUNA, 1930

Oil on canvas, 36 x 40 inches
Collection of William Selman

IN THE TWILIGHT OF HIS CAREER, Kleitsch focused on painting the beehive of activity on Laguna's downtown streets. The transformation from village life to a more cosmopolitan city atmosphere was daunting, and Kleitsch was determined to record this dramatic change. Several of his street scenes focus on the heavily trafficked intersection of Forest and Park avenues as they merged with Coast Boulevard. In the lower left quadrant of *Laguna Avenue and Hotel Laguna*, the White Café is directly behind the girl in white and to the left of the street sign. Across the street is the Isch Building, a white structure with arches that is still standing. A new landmark, the Laguna Hotel, identifiable by its distinctive tower, opened in 1930 and is still operating. Similar to his other paintings of downtown Laguna, Kleitsch has included summarily treated abstract figures in this scene.

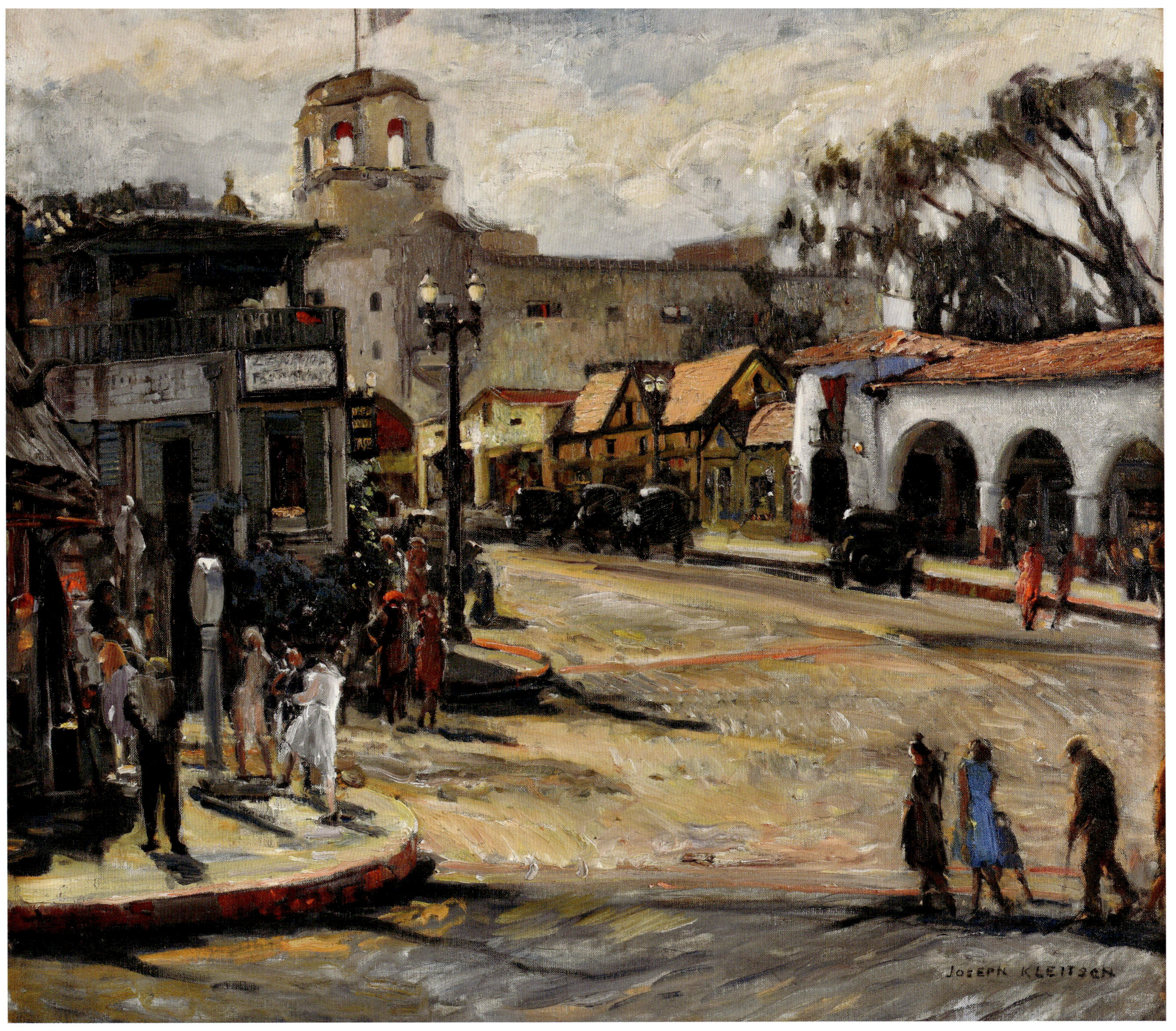
JOSEPH KLEITSCH

LAGUNA ON A CLOUDY DAY (MAIN BEACH), c. 1930

Oil on canvas, 36 x 40 inches
Private Collection, from the Estate of Pearl Martin

A DARK, CLOUDY DAY AT THE BEACH is not unusual for Laguna's sometimes-mercurial weather, especially in late afternoon. For a change of pace and palette, Kleitsch composed a scene on an overcast, windy day at Main Beach, looking toward the nearby mountains. Taking advantage of the dark, threatening clouds and wind-bent trees, the artist set up his easel on the sandy beach to capture an impending rainstorm. In this view, he painted the ensembles of figures gathered on the beach and carefully delineated key structures along the old beach boardwalk, beginning with the white building with arched windows, Café las Ondas. The ochre-colored building in the center left is the Laguna bathhouse, and the three-storied white building with the red-tiled roof and tower-like structure is an apartment building. As an addition to this graphic scene, the artist painted strands of seaweed across the sand.

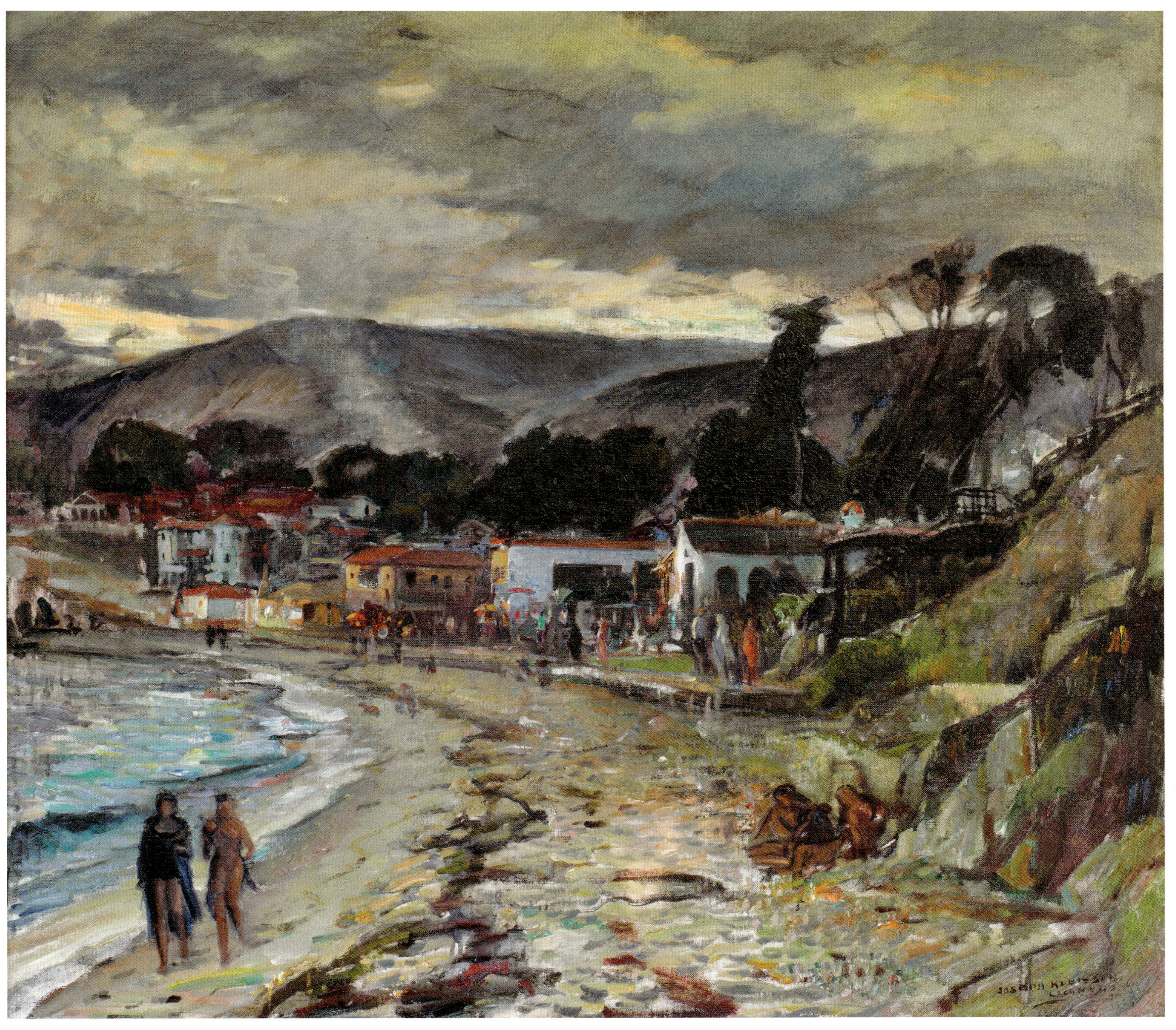

NUDES, c. 1929–30

Oil on canvas, 20 ½ x 18 inches
Collection of Linda and David O'Hoy

THIS SMALL STUDY OF THE INTERIOR of Laguna's Main Beach bathhouse displays the artist's playful and perverse sense of humor. He has inserted himself, or perhaps a male stranger, in the women's quarters of the bathhouse. Is he a voyeur, or an unidentified person just enjoying the women while they disrobe? Because of Kleitsch's background and affinity for women, it is not surprising that he found humor in this setting. His rapid brushstrokes of various colors abstractly handled draw the viewer's eyes from the man bent over with his head turned away from the three undulating female nudes—perhaps representing the mythical Three Graces—looking at him in shock and distain. One woman with an outstretched arm appears to be closing a door to separate them from the lone, seated male.

Several interpretations of this study have been advanced, but it still remains a conundrum. Perhaps, literally, Kleitsch wished to show both interior rooms of the bathhouse, one for women and the other for men, to complete his rendering of the Main Beach bathhouse. Another interpretation that has been proffered is that this is a gay male who resists the three females, who seemingly tempt him by what appears to be a sexual proposition. It is a well-known fact that Laguna, with its seaside location, had a significant gay community that was woven into local society. Just as Kleitsch recorded the physical changes in the appearance of the town, here he seems to address a conspicuous aspect of the changed social fabric of Laguna, the presence and acceptance of a gay community by 1930.

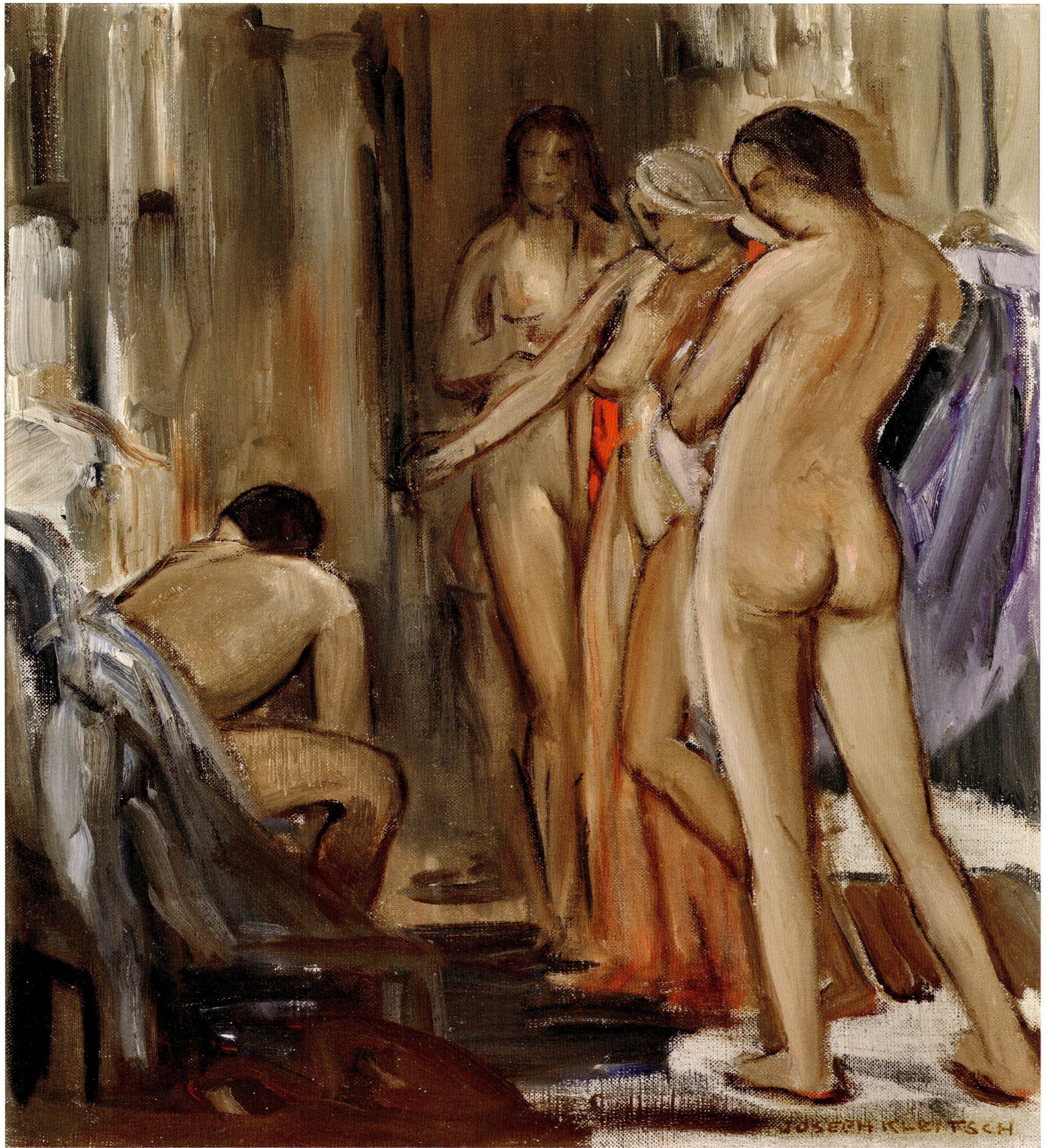
JOSEPH KLEITSCH

OCEAN FRONT—MAIN BEACH, LAGUNA, c. 1929–30

Oil on canvas, 36 x 40 inches
Collection of Stephen P. Diamond, M.D.

KLEITSCH, MUCH LIKE THE East Coast impressionists William Glackens (1870–1938) and Edward Potthast (1857–1927), was attracted to the liveliness of the beach scene, with its throngs of bathers and sun worshippers in their motley bathing costumes. Two late Kleitsch paintings of bathers, *Sunday, Laguna Beach,* 1929, and *Ocean Front—Main Beach, Laguna,* of about 1929–30, forecast a freer, more consistent, expressive approach to abstraction. The view presented by *Ocean Front—Main Beach, Laguna* is confined to the bathhouse and adjacent human activity. In capturing this scene, the artist set up his easel at the intersection of Ocean Avenue and South Coast Boulevard, looking toward Main Beach through an opening in the buildings at the foot of Ocean Avenue. A historical photograph of the Laguna Beach bathhouse exterior demonstrates how literally he represented the building. On the right, adjacent to the bathhouse, is the sandy pathway to the beach, and next to it the board-and-plank sidewalk. In Kleitsch's rendition, bathers promenade near the bathhouse with their colorful garb and paraphernalia, energized by the view of the Pacific Ocean. By narrowing the pathway, Kleitsch creates a tunnel-like effect that draws the viewer's eye to the light and the bluish-green waters beyond. Moving with purpose through the bazaar-like setting, the bathers glide toward the beach and its busy concession stand. A towel-draped woman on the left in a *contrapposto* stance recalls a classical Roman figure wearing a toga. Like another painting, *Café las Ondas* (p. 83), Kleitsch places an amusing phantom figure seated in a car in the lower right corner to reinforce the composition's diagonal forward thrust. As in his other late pictures, Kleitsch has introduced baroque elements and compositional devices to increase the image's complexity.

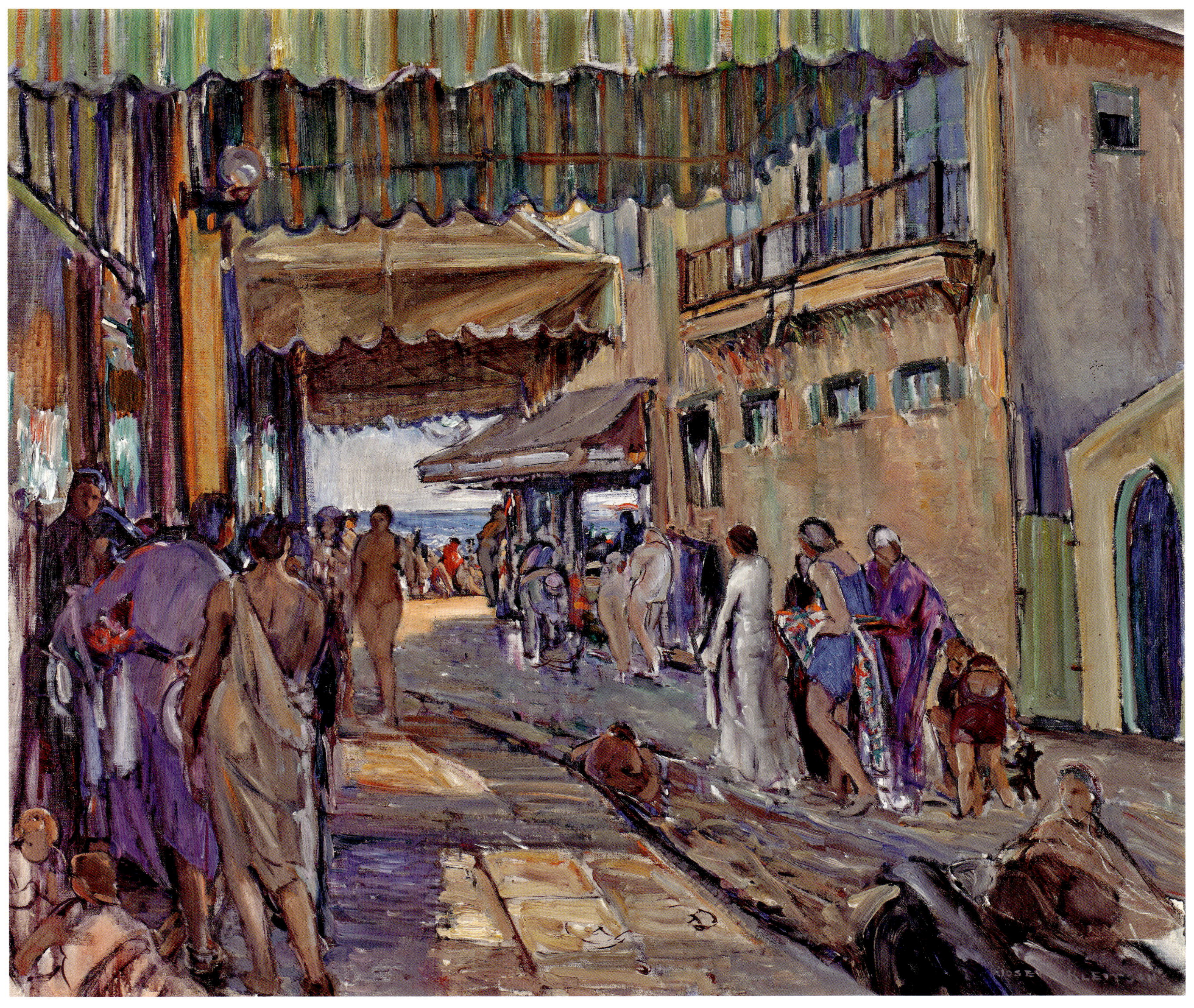

LAGUNA ROAD II, c. 1929–30

Oil on canvas, 36 x 40 inches
Private Collection

DURING 1924, KLEITSCH PAINTED a prodigious number of scenes of Old Laguna, in the morning, noon, and evening light, showing the original structures that lined its dusty roads. He painted Laguna's ubiquitous eucalyptus trees in sun and shadow, blown by the Pacific breezes, or with their golden leaves hanging in the heat of summer. Kleitsch's vigorous brush, loaded with myriad rich colors, and his manipulation of the ever-changing light vividly evoke the old village. Kleitsch did not limit his efforts to any one area of Laguna but painted the coastline and shores with their ubiquitous bathers, the village and its environs, the canyons, and the surrounding hills. Driven by the desire to record the village before its dramatic urban transformation, he shifted his easel frequently from place to place.

These paintings were intended for the Kleitsch Academy of Art, but unfortunately, his premature death precluded this objective. After he completed his 1924 *Laguna Road* painting (p. 37), he felt compelled to paint another version, as the original had been sold to the city of Laguna. The second is a close facsimile, with infinitesimal variations, a broader brushstroke, and brighter hues. In certain areas of the later version, he was moving toward abstraction, in contrast to the tighter, more graphic rendering of the earlier painting.

Since many of the landmarks had been removed because of the city's rapid growth, he had to rely on the 1924 version of the painting as his model. For the earlier picture, he stood at a spot on the inland side of Coast Boulevard across from the Old Hotel Laguna. The eucalyptus grove was later removed to accommodate the new Hotel Laguna, built in 1930. In both versions, Laguna Avenue crosses over the heads of the two foreground figures; the white structure known as the Isch Building is at the center of the picture, immediately above the parked car; Coast Boulevard bends off to the left at the intersection, with Forest Avenue at center right; the White House is the third building on the right, with the light-colored façade and awning; the hill in the background is now part of Laguna Coast Wilderness Park.

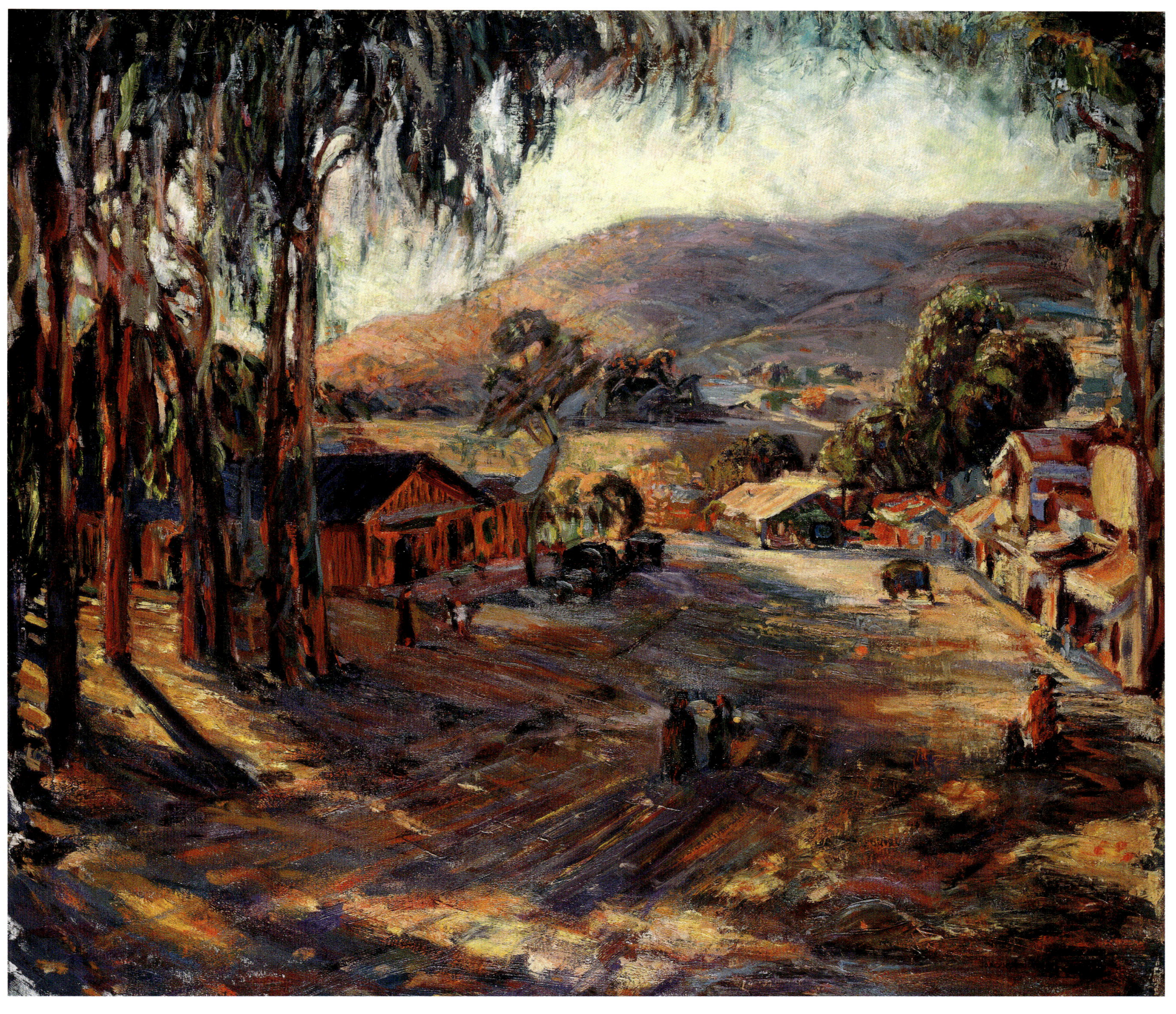

EL PASEO, 1928–29

Oil on canvas, 30 x 40 inches
Private Collection

IN THE SUMMER MONTHS, El Paseo, an alley by Hotel Laguna, bustled with throngs of bathers on their way to Main Beach. By placing his easel on the western end of the alley, Kleitsch chose to depict the rear of the board-and-batten buildings fronting the old Main Beach boardwalk and the recently graded area at the end of the street. The Old Hotel Laguna, built by Joseph and Catherine Yoch, had been razed to accommodate the construction of the modern Laguna Hotel, to be opened in 1930. The blue gum eucalyptus trees bending in the wind graphically portray the frequent offshore winds and provide an attractive foil for the old structures. The small cluster of figures on the street, summarily treated with broad brushstrokes of rich color, manifest the painting style that Kleitsch adopted after his European trip and suggest the uncomplicated nature of daily life in the village.

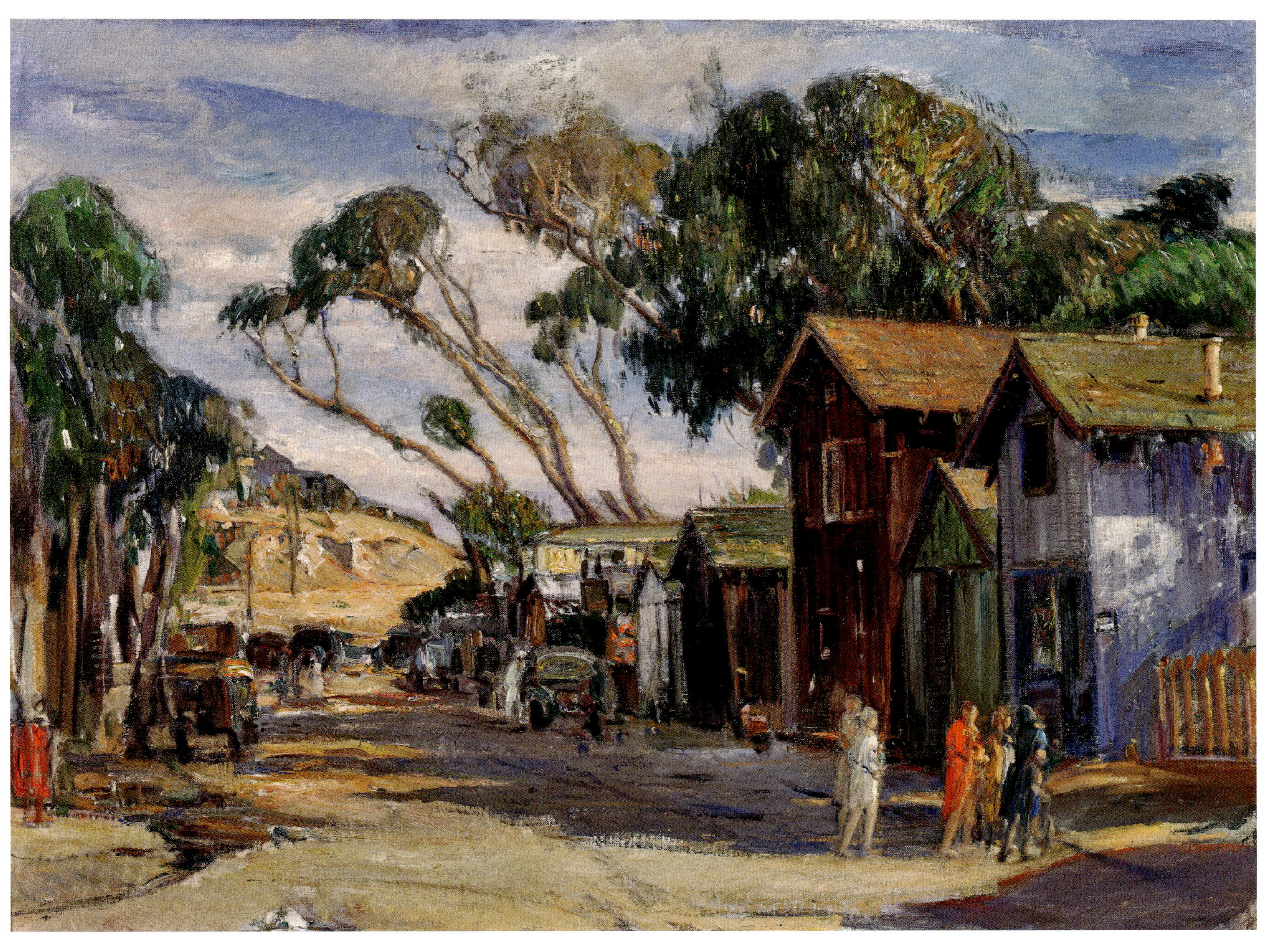

ENCHANTMENT, 1922

Oil on canvas, 22 x 18 ¼ inches
Private Collection

IN THE EARLY 1920S, Edna was kept exceedingly busy with multiple chores, while Kleitsch was committed to his new contract with the Stendahl Galleries, enlarging his repertory in order to fulfill his obligation for additional paintings. Whereas the dealer collected 50 percent from sales, Edna was given the opportunity to obtain a 15 percent commission for her outside sales efforts. As the family had moved into larger quarters at the Turner House, near the general store in Laguna, she found herself very involved, along with taking care of their youngster.

Taking a respite from all those chores, she often wandered off to one of the many coves along the oceanfront to sit surrounded by looming, craggy rocks, shown here with daubs of color, dabbling her feet in a pool of water. Alone with her thoughts, she could enjoy some quiet meditation, as the change and direction of her life was at times overwhelming, and the mild weather was an opportunity to take advantage of this setting. The artist evidently followed her and captured his wife in an animated, plein-air painting, full of vigorous brushwork and vibrant color, which he titled *Enchantment.* Obviously, he was enchanted by her reverie in this sheltered and quiet spot, away from the teeming humanity surrounding them. Edna is wearing her iconic red jacket, which appears in other paintings by the artist, like the exceptional *Red and Green* (p. 107). He selected this favorite painting of his wife to exhibit at the Laguna Beach Art Association exhibition gallery on October 20, 1922.

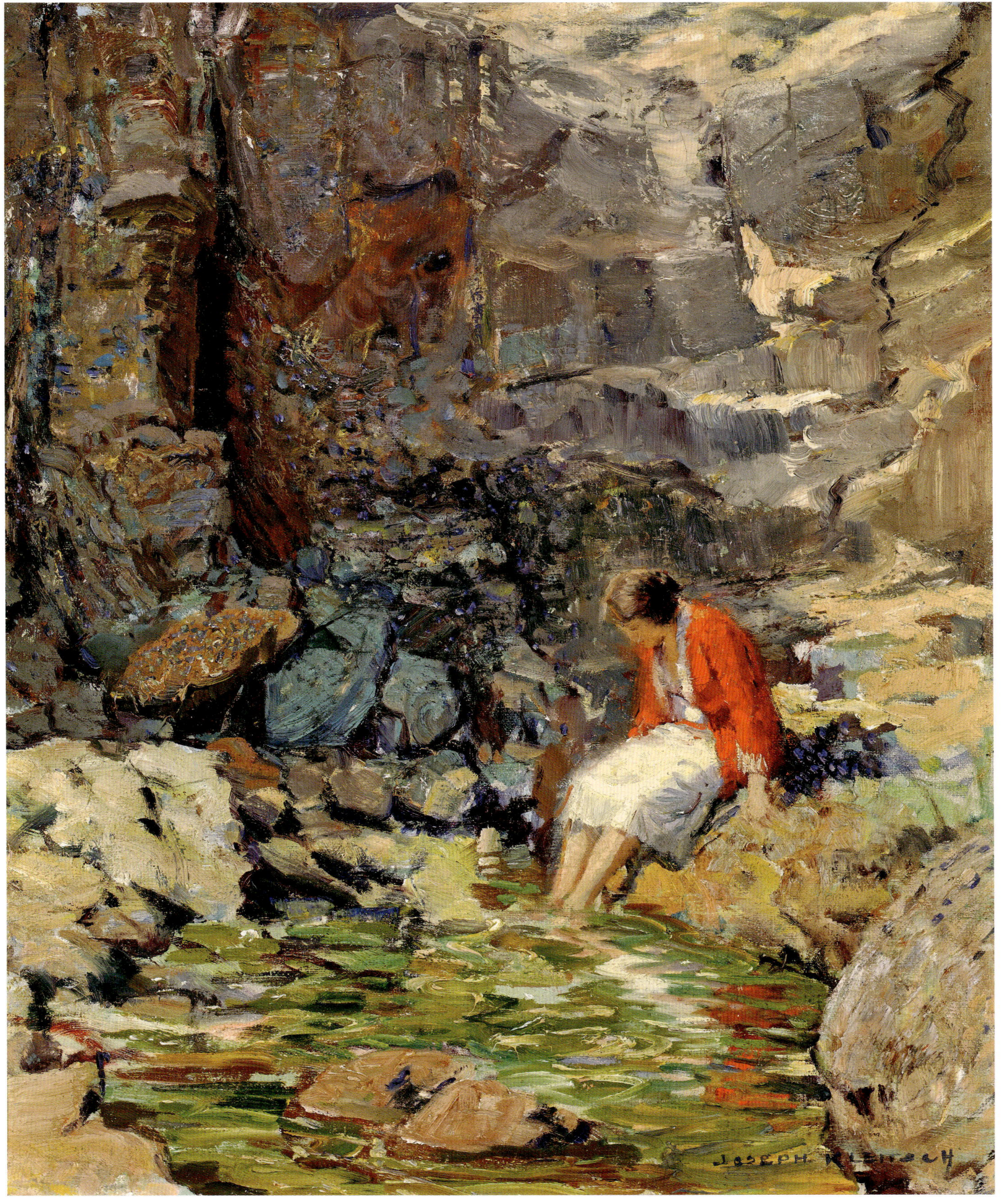
JOSEPH

UNDER THE EUCALYPTUS TREES, 1922

Oil on canvas, 45 x 35 inches
Private Collection

KLEITSCH EXHIBITED *Under the Eucalyptus Trees*, painted in 1922, at the Third Annual Art Exhibit of Occidental College, held at the Stendahl Galleries April 19–25, 1928. When Laguna's first modern hostel, La Casa del Camino, opened on February 1, 1929, it featured a display of Kleitsch's prized landscape paintings of Old Laguna, showcasing the "easeful days of good roads, good water, gas and electricity." *Los Angeles Times* art critic Antony Anderson praised *Under the Eucalyptus Trees,* one of his favorite paintings "interpreted by a painter-poet" (*South Coast News*, January 25, 1929).

This colorful painting shows Edna wearing her iconic red jacket and shading herself with a white parasol on a very hot summer day, walking under leafy eucalyptus trees that form an archway to the approach of the Old Hotel—razed in 1929 and replaced by the new Laguna Hotel.

The eucalyptus grove seen in the painting was later removed in order to accommodate the building of the new hotel. Eucalyptus trees brought to America years before were harvested as railroad ties for the rapidly expanding rail system. The ubiquitous trees had been planted throughout Southern California, but their numbers have been significantly reduced by the rapid expansion and development of older communities, like Laguna.

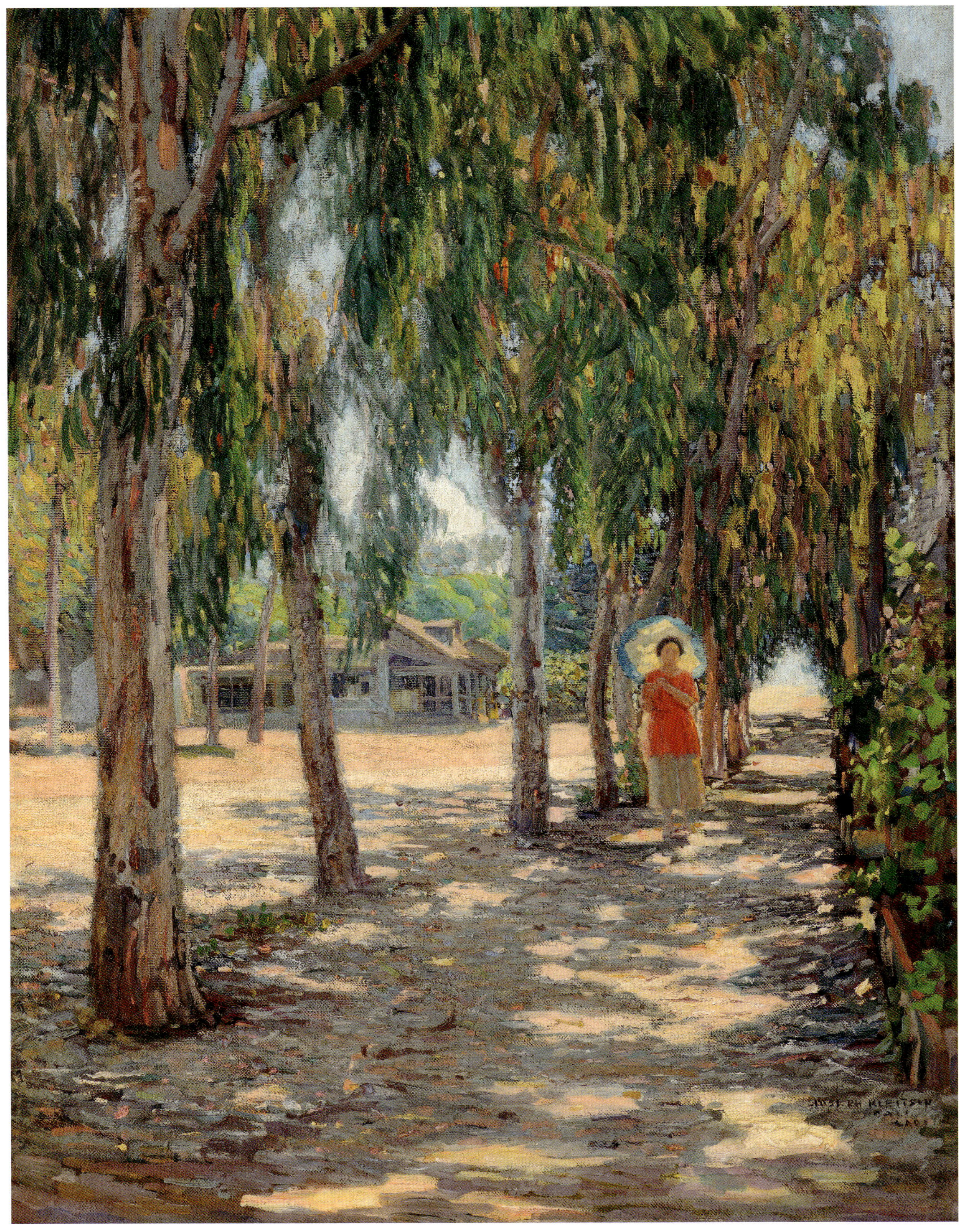

COMRADES, c. 1928

Oil on canvas, 40 x 36 inches
Collection of Ken Mizushima

IN THIS CHARMING PAINTING, Kleitsch vividly brings into focus his extraordinary ability to master color, composition, and portraiture. His son Eugene and a younger friend casually posed for the artist in the brilliant morning light, most likely on their way to school. Employing a colorful background of grasses, flowers, and trees, Kleitsch has captured the two boys with a full impressionistic brush of bright color, as the dappled light reflects on their clothing and faces. By tilting the background, he brought the boys into the foreground plane as the focal point of the composition. In doing so, the artist had to crop out the legs and feet in order to focus on their highlighted young faces. Kleitsch has realistically articulated their features, even though the vigorous impressionistic brushwork is quite evident. The red lips and rosy cheeks indicate that the boys had probably been running, as portrayed by the artist, in order not to be late for school. Eugene and his friend are wearing typical casual boys' clothing of jeans and long-sleeved shirts, rolled up at the elbows, which was the uniform of the day.

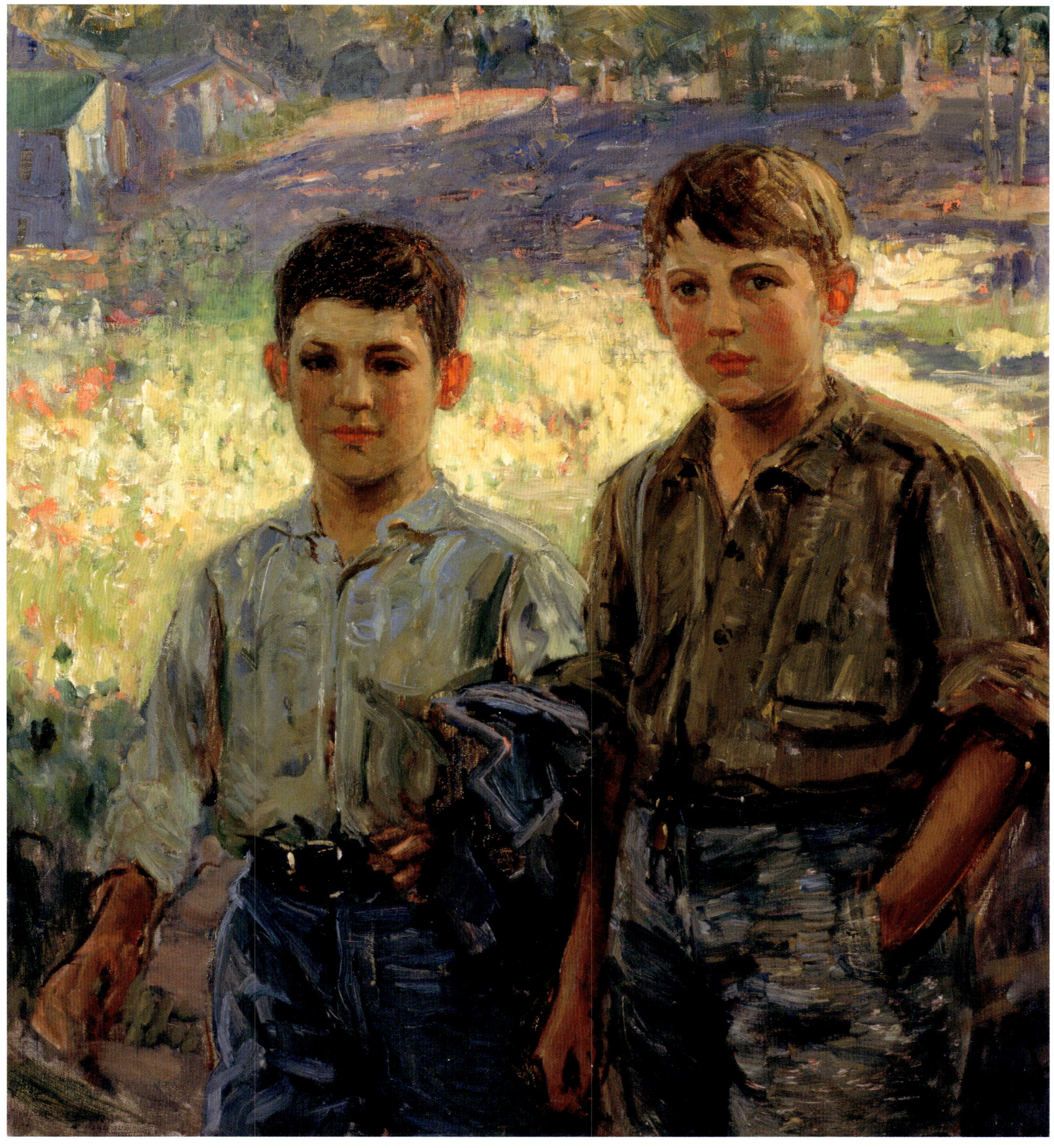

BEACHCOMBERS, c. 1928

Oil on canvas, 26 x 30 inches
Courtesy of The Kelley Gallery and George Stern Fine Arts

BEACHCOMBERS MIGHT BE CONSIDERED a companion piece to the painting *Comrades* (p. 101), in which Kleitsch depicts his son and a friend. Although both paintings are undated, Eugene appears to be three years older in these paintings than in *The Story Teller,* which is dated 1925. In *Comrades* and *Beachcombers* the two figures are wearing typical teenage boys' clothing, which might indicate that the paintings were done within a short period of time; this may also be reaffirmed by the boys' physical anatomy. In *Beachcombers,* however, Kleitsch does employ a palette of more vibrant colors and expressive, swirling brushstrokes.

Here the boys are seated in a secluded cove, almost surrounded by bulky, multicolored rocks, with a narrow opening that provides a glimpse of the ocean beyond. There are many coves along Laguna's shores, with each having an almost seductive appeal. If one were to guess, it appears that this setting is a cove near Arch Beach. Kleitsch had painted the arches at a nearby location with the same rugged, lively brushstrokes as seen here in *Beachcombers*. In similar fashion, the kaleidoscope of colors applied to the canvas does animate the background setting for the boys, who are seated closely together. The space, while small and cramped, does accommodate the two teenage boys resting and meditating on the scenic wonders of their environment. The rocks seem to roil in movement, and the bluish-green ocean echoes their message. The small object in the foreground is a glass bowl used by the boys to catch some of the fascinating small sea creatures that are usually available in narrow coves. The hideaway setting and the wonderful colorful portraits vividly capture the mood. As with his other portraits, Kleitsch's special talents portray the boys' expressions and features in a manner that is unlike that of any of his contemporaries.

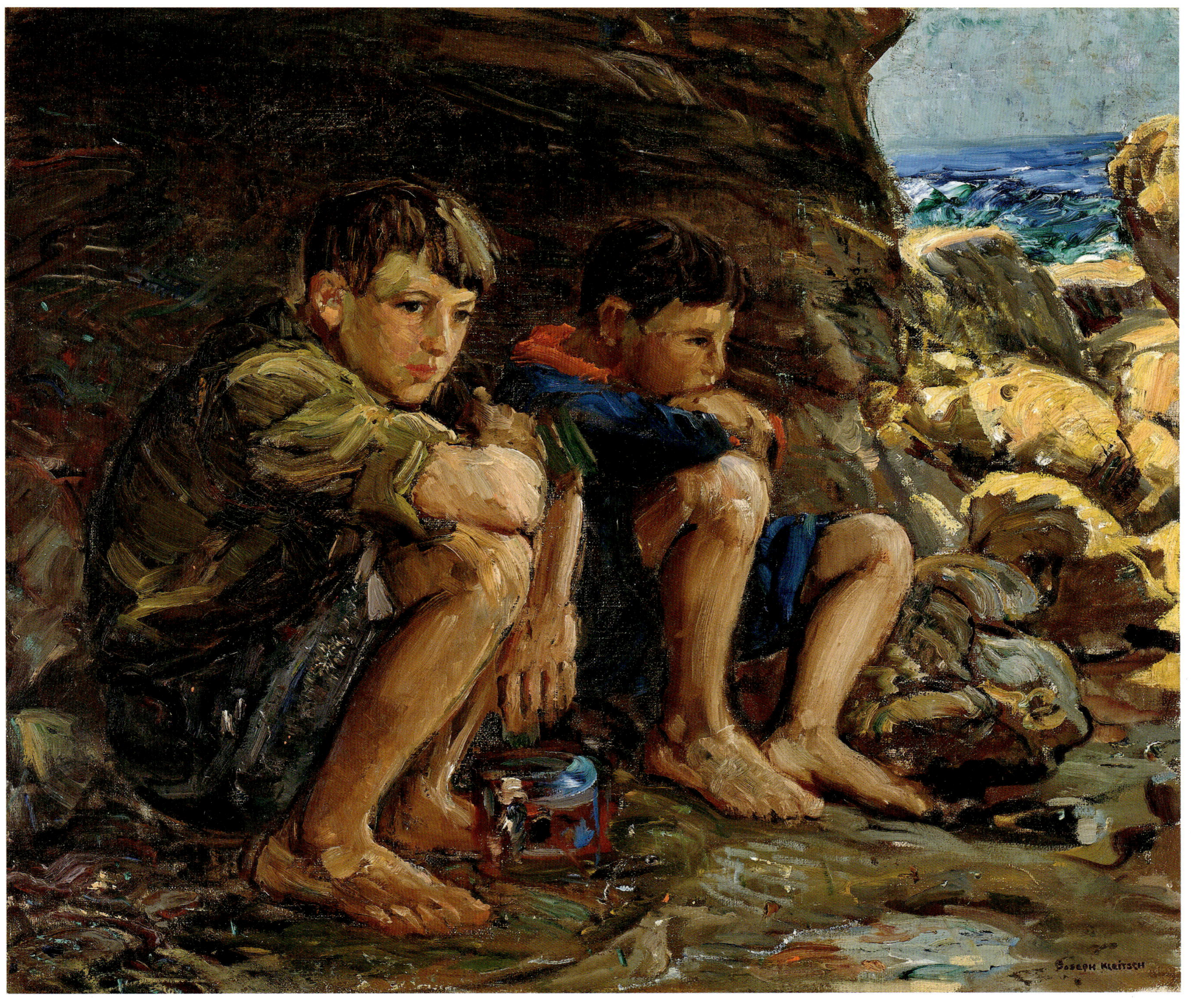
JOSEPH KLEITSCH

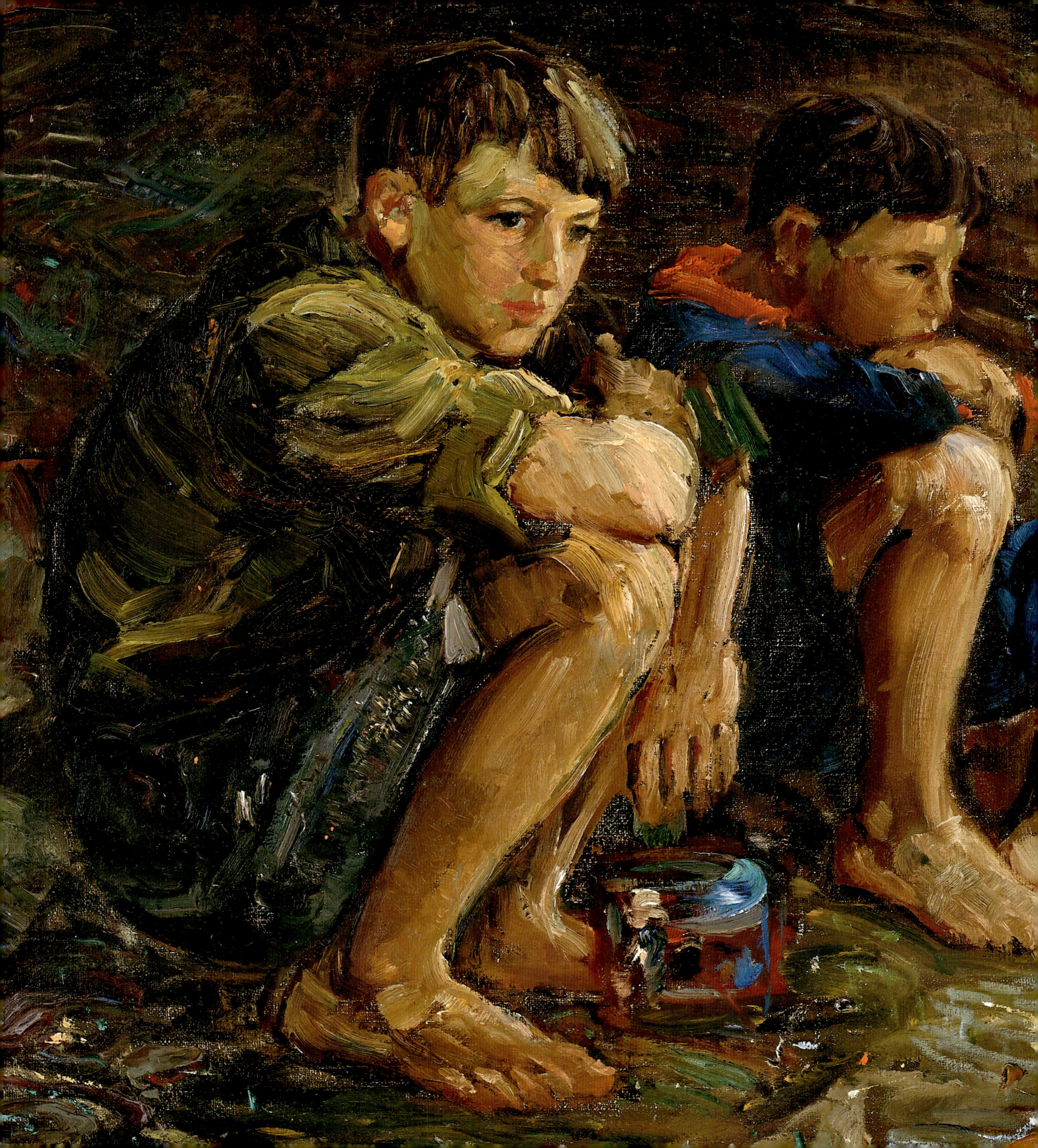

Eugene was born in 1915, a year after Kleitsch and Edna's marriage in Chicago. He grew up as an only child, Edna having lost her younger son in 1921, three days after his birth. As seen in his father's loving portraits, Eugene seems to have enjoyed the rewards of youth. However, after the artist's untimely death, in November 1931, the tide turned for Eugene. He and his mother struggled to survive financially after the loss of a husband and father. Eugene began to lean on his mother for support and seemed to lack an enjoyment of life; he was thought of as strange and possibly mentally disturbed. However, Robert Kleitsch, a cousin of his father, disputes this story. As his business partner in Chicago, Robert said Eugene was a creative, skilled photographer but unfortunately also an alcoholic. An early photograph shows the two of them together in Chicago. The details of Eugene's life after that are very sketchy; he returned to Laguna to live with his mother, but after her death ended up in a state hospital, where he died of a heart attack.

The pictorial record of Eugene that his father has provided gives us a more pleasant impression of a young teenage boy. The trio of paintings—*The Story Teller, Comrades*, and *Beachcombers*—are special in depicting the pleasant and enjoyable youthful days of that period.

RED AND GREEN (MISSION SAN JUAN CAPISTRANO), 1923

Oil on canvas, 36 x 40 inches
The Irvine Museum

IN MID-DECEMBER OF 1922, Kleitsch began a painting tour of the historic missions in the Southland. The one that caught his eye with the most possibilities was Mission San Juan Capistrano, which he frequently revisited to sketch and paint. This old adobe mission and its colorful gardens provided numerous subjects for his brush. In July 1923, Kleitsch began an extended sketching tour to San Juan Capistrano. His keen sense of color responded to the colorful gardens, profuse with vegetation, and the subtle attractiveness of the rough adobe walls and cloisters. An exceptional and striking painting that resulted from this trip is *Red and Green,* which demonstrates his response to this colorful and historic site.

Just as in *The Oriental Shop* (p. 65), riotous, vibrant colors appear in this figural landscape. In the mission's front garden, Edna, in her familiar red jacket, shades her eyes as a young Mexican girl kneels nearby among the flowering plants. The soft adobe color of the mission's south wing contrasts with the figures, the colorful garden, and the large, leafy pepper tree. The strong sunlight highlights the two figures, and the artist evokes a sense of the deep religious significance of the old mission's faded grandeur and tranquility. This was one of the many views of the front garden and south wing made on the trip. Kleitsch was now known as an accomplished impressionist plein-air artist.

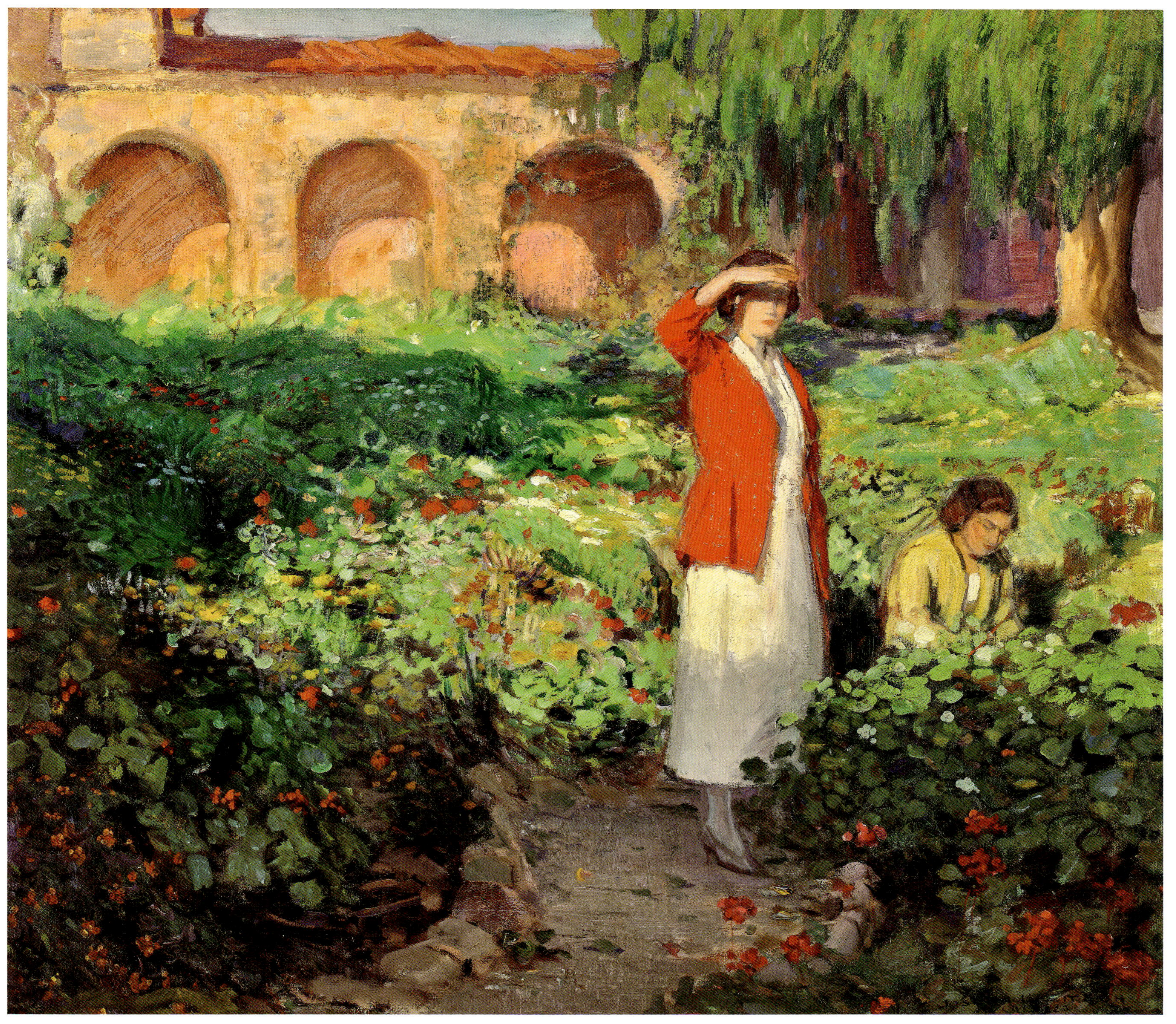

EL PEÓN [JOSÉ JUAN OLIVARES], SAN JUAN CAPISTRANO, 1923

Oil on canvas, 30 x 25 inches
Collection of James W. and Sarah T. Miller

IN NOVEMBER 1924, Kleitsch submitted a number of his mission paintings for an exhibition at the Art Center of the Painters and Sculptors Club in Los Angeles; he was awarded a silver medal for his entry of *El Peón* (also known as *José Juan Olivares*) for its fine "characterization." Although some critics questioned the artist's "lack of care" with the foreground details, the unidentified subject undoubtedly was a local laborer involved in the restoration of the Capistrano mission. The identity of the subject here and in *Old Man Yorba* was later confirmed and is therefore no longer a mystery. The most characteristic feature of Kleitsch's treatment of his male character is a forceful, but somewhat rough, irregular technique. The face is deeply wrinkled and weather-beaten, and the large, expressive hands recall the Dutch master Joseph Israel (1824–1911), whose artwork Kleitsch carefully studied when it was exhibited at Moulton & Ricketts Galleries in Chicago in 1924.

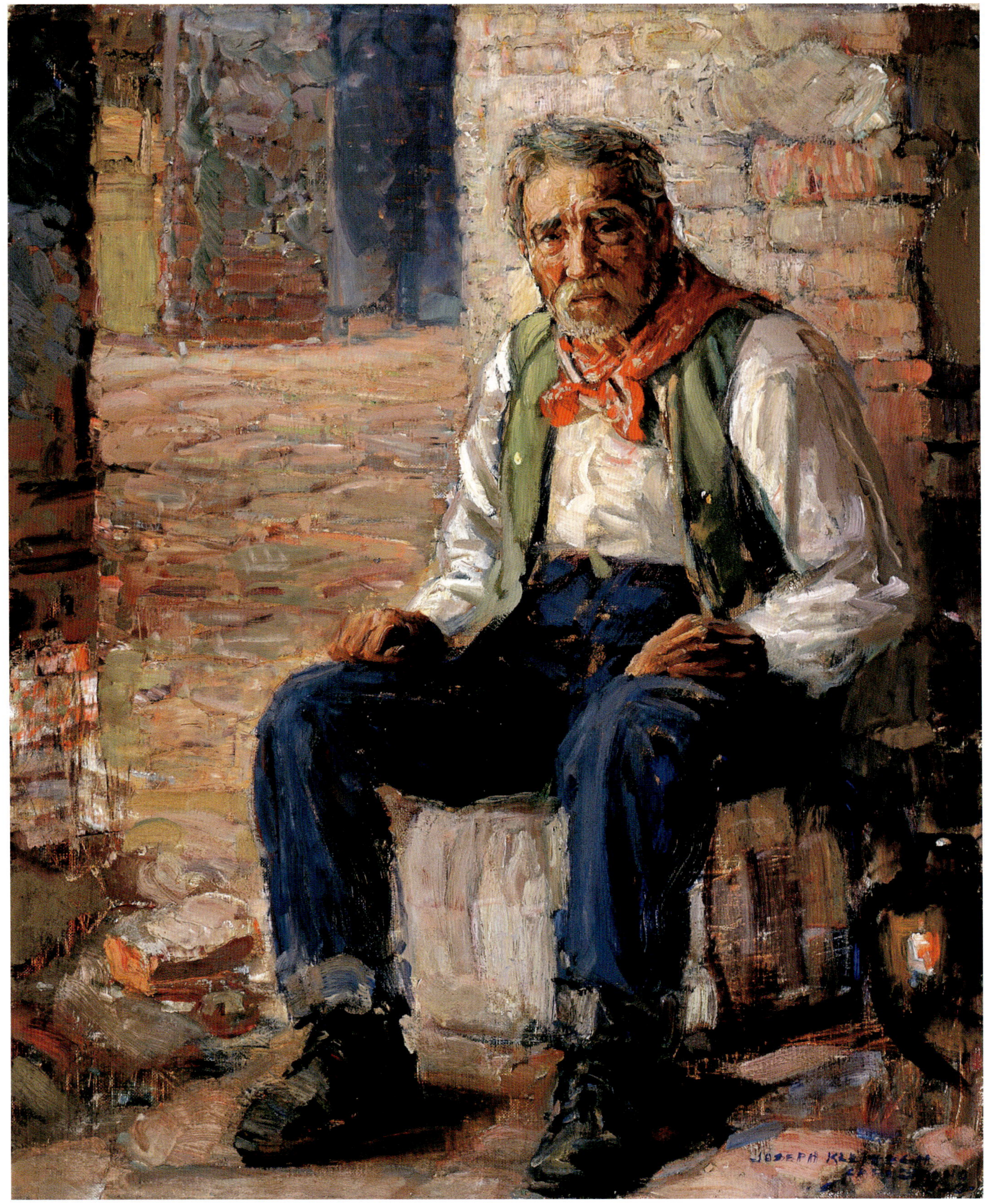
JOSEPH

THE STORY TELLER (EUGENE AND EL PEÓN [JOSÉ JUAN OLIVARES]), 1925

Oil on canvas, 18 x 22 inches
Collection of William Selman

HERE KLEITSCH HAS POSED the elderly José Juan, patriarch of San Juan Capistrano, with the artist's son, Eugene, who appears to be intently listening to the old man's story. They are seated in one of the mission's arcades, adjacent to a rough, adobe brick wall with a variety of colors. From Kleitsch's visual interpretation, it is evident that the mission was overdue for a restoration of its irregular, rough adobe brick surfaces. In 1924, Kleitsch had painted a portrait of Father St. John O'Sullivan, the resident priest who was largely responsible for the restoration of the mission. Father O'Sullivan also initiated the renovation of the damaged Serra Chapel, built a new mission school, created the flower gardens, and installed several fountains. Using his forceful personality, he encouraged writers and artists to carry his vision of the mission to the outside world through their writings, art, and lectures.

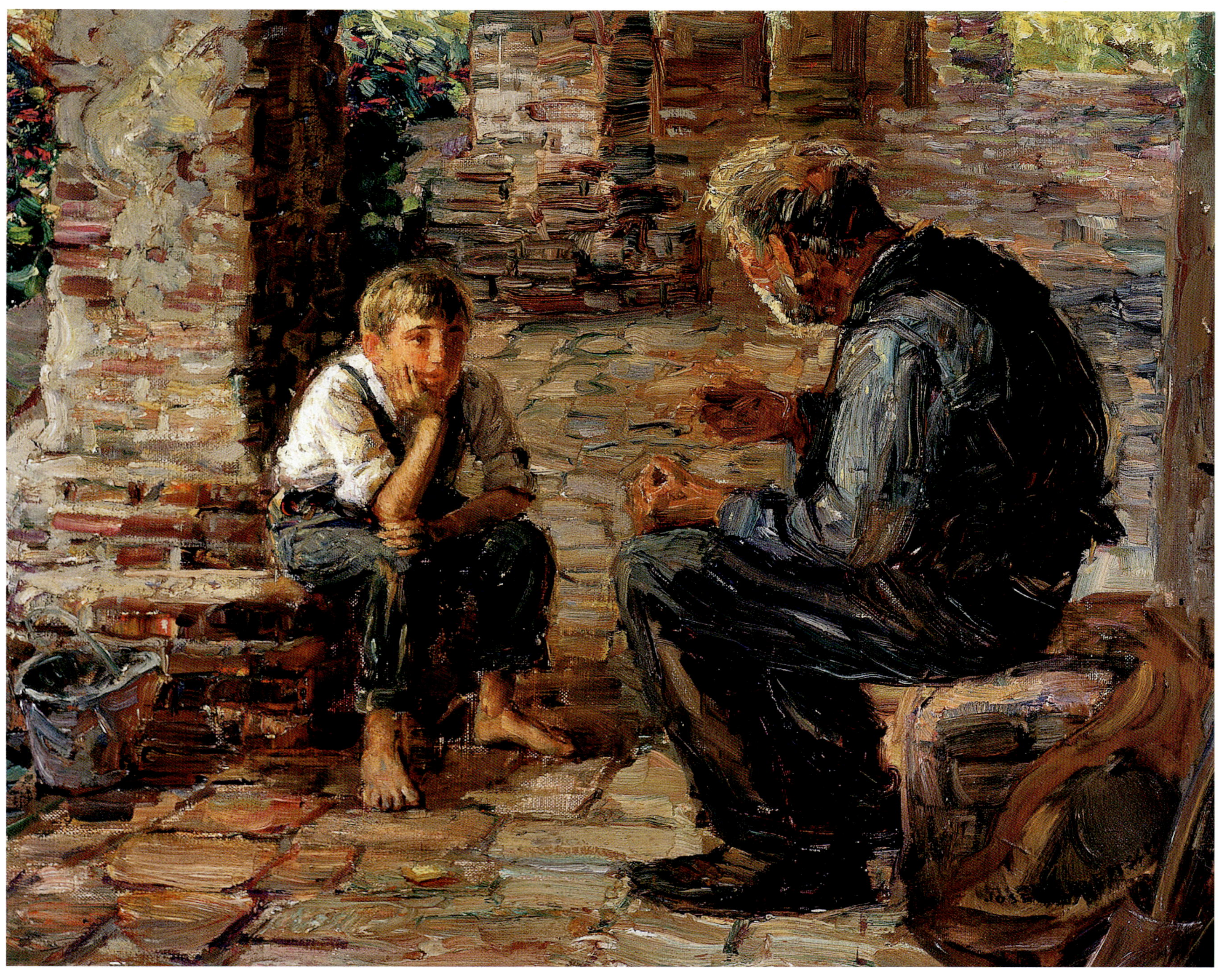

Curiosity (Mission San Juan Capistrano), 1924

Oil on canvas, 25 x 30 inches
Collection Mr. and Mrs. Thomas B. Stiles II

AFTER DISCOVERING THE BEAUTY of the faded mission and gardens at San Juan Capistrano, Kleitsch became less interested in portraiture and more interested in the inclusion of figures in the landscape. One of these figural paintings is *Curiosity,* depicting two little girls from Capistrano intensely absorbed in the mysterious contents of the artist's palette and paint box. Kleitsch captures the youth, vitality, and beauty of the two girls with spontaneous, impressionistic brushstrokes in strong and bright harmonious colors. Whether the artist actually observed this scene or had the girls pose for the composition is a matter of conjecture. The young Hispanic girl with dark hair and long curls, whose face is turned toward the viewer, has been identified as Eustalia Soto of San Juan Capistrano, who later served as a guide at the mission. She also appears in several of Kleitsch's other mission pictures, like *Going to Church* (*Sunday Morning*, p. 115). Eustalia's family, originally from Texas, had moved to San Juan Capistrano around 1900.

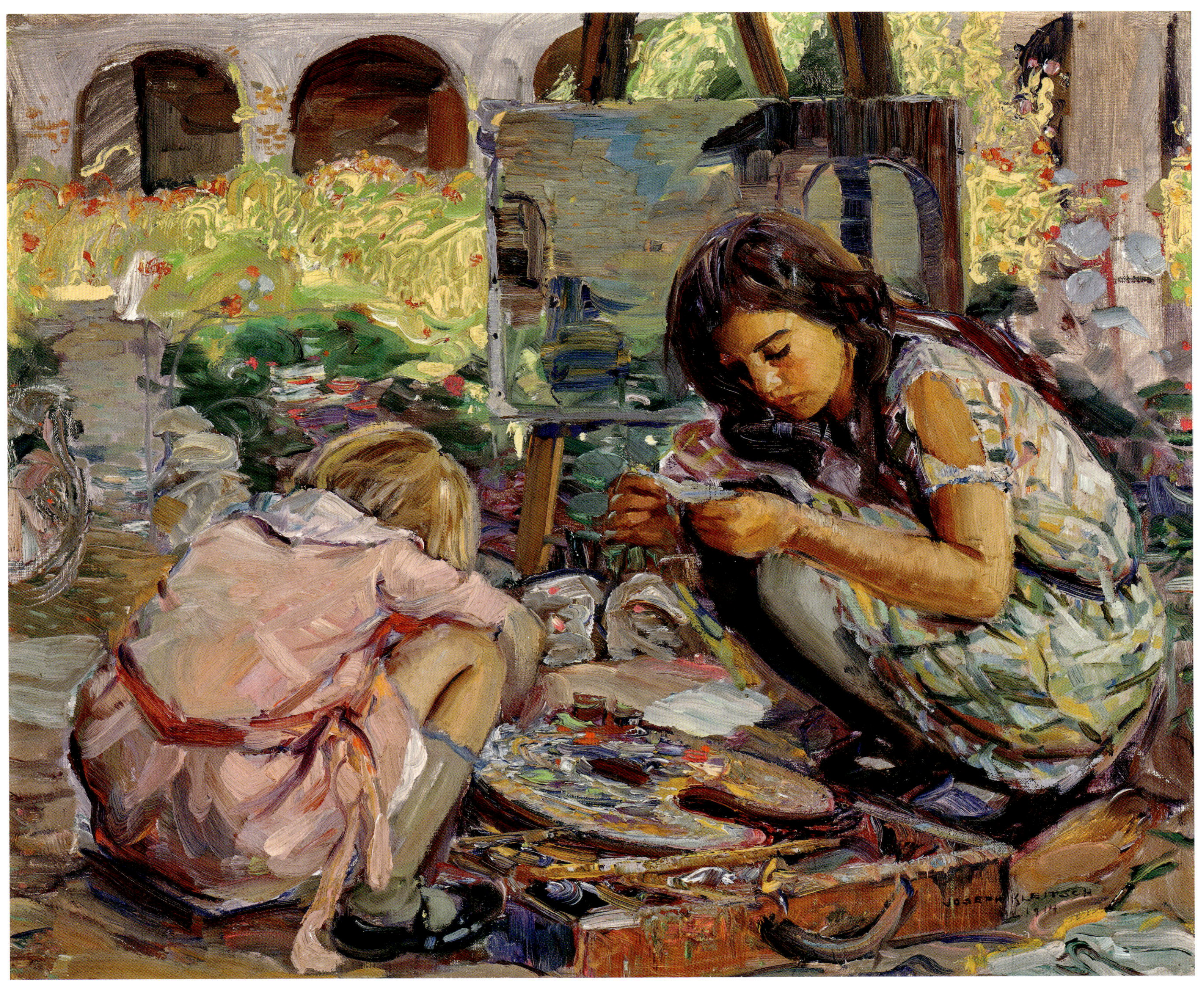
JOSEPH KLEITSCH

GOING TO CHURCH (SUNDAY MORNING), CAPISTRANO, 1924

Oil on canvas, 40 x 36 inches
Private Collection

IN THE SUMMER OF 1924, Kleitsch took the opportunity to repeatedly record the mission with personal affection through a series of paintings. In the original version of *Going to Church,* Kleitsch captured worshippers about to attend Sunday Mass at the newly restored chapel of Father O'Sullivan. He skillfully portrays two young Mexican girls in their Sunday best, accompanied by their parents. At a later date, in an attempt to improve the composition, the artist removed the parents looking on in the upper right quadrant, making the colorfully costumed girls the focal point of the painting. Kleitsch's use of vibrant colors and multitextured surfaces enlivens the mood of this somewhat somber setting.

The two Hispanic girls have been identified as Lulu (Dora) Avila and Eustalia Soto (to the viewer's right, with long curls). Lulu is wearing a Spanish shawl and sports a hairstyle of the 1920s. Eustalia—who appears in several other mission paintings by Kleitsch, like *Curiosity* (p. 113)—wears Western attire. Both girls served as tour guides at Mission San Juan Capistrano during the 1920s.

Lulu was from a very distinguished early California family; she was a descendant of Don Juan Avila, who had established Rancho Niguel (Laguna Niguel) in 1830. Her mother was a member of the Yorba family, one of the first families in San Juan Capistrano; they had been granted one of the first ranchos in California. These two families were the most prominent in the county and in San Juan Capistrano in the early 1800s. Later in life, Lulu married Robert Howe, an engineer, and they appear to have moved to Venice, California. Eustalia Soto (nicknamed "Estolia") was from the Soto family of Texas, who had moved to San Juan Capistrano around 1900. The story goes that Eustalia met a man in town and left San Juan Capistrano sometime in the early 1930s.

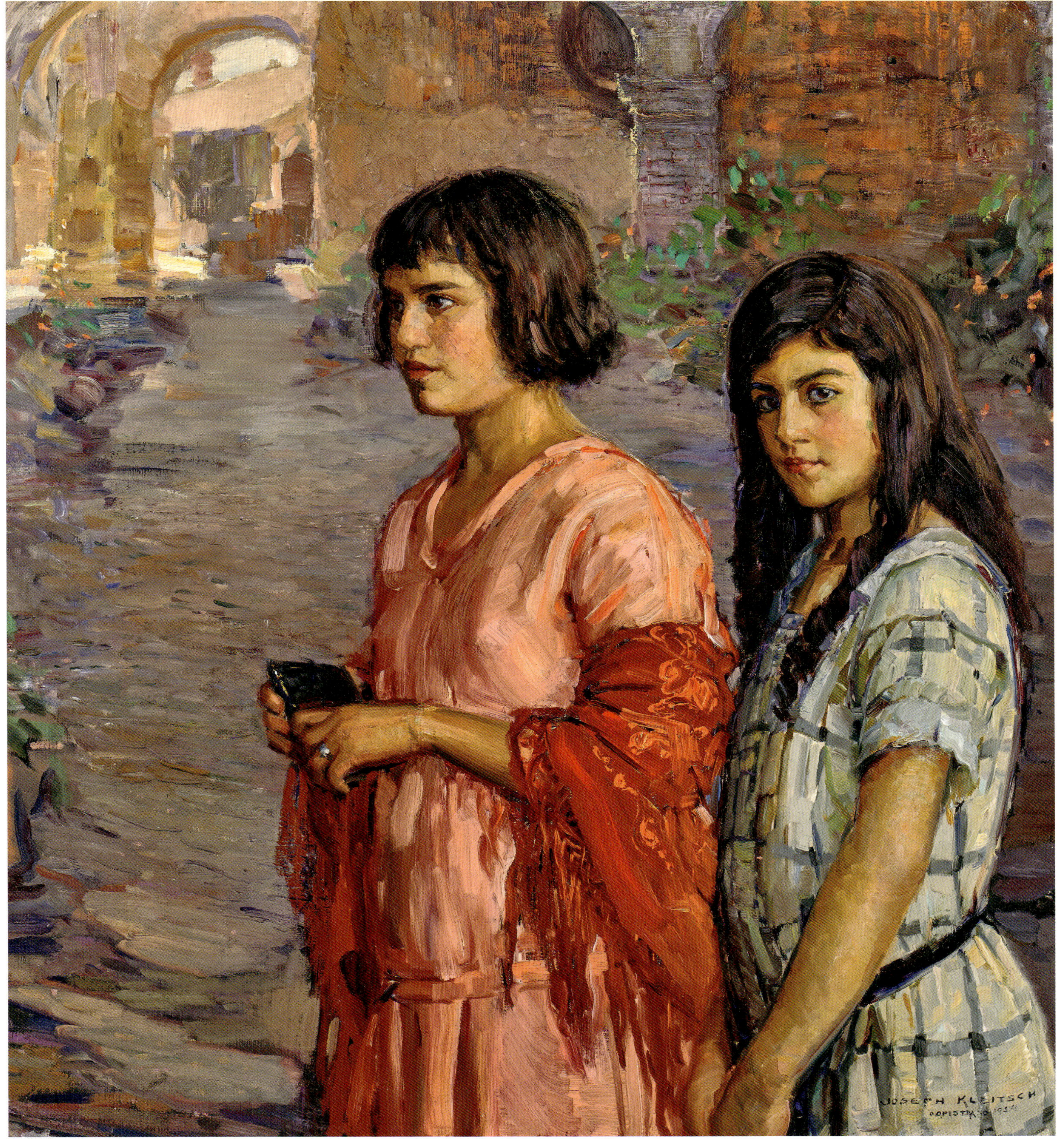
JOSEPH KLEITSCH

PARIS, 1926

Oil on canvas, 36 x 36 inches
Collection of W. Donald Head, Old Grandview Ranch

KLEITSCH WENT ON AN EXTENDED TRIP to Europe, arriving in Paris in February 1926. He resided briefly at the Hotel California, just off the Champs-Élysées at 16 rue de Berri. There he painted a casual, almost full-length self-portrait using a mirror, giving us some insight into one of the vehicles he employed for painting his self-portraits. He also used the photograph as a vehicle, as evidenced by his 1909 self-portrait (p. 127).

For this painting, the artist looked out from his hotel window over the rooftops of the area and painted an aerial perspective of the city. In this view, he depicts the movement of the small dark figures below, the pathways, and the streets receding upward toward the tilted background. The tiled roofs are punctuated with vivid reddish-orange color, and the mansard and other types of roofs are painted in brown. The few sketchy, slender green trees below and the white sidings of the few buildings in front relieve the darkness of the scene, contrasted by a sliver of the blue Seine at the top.

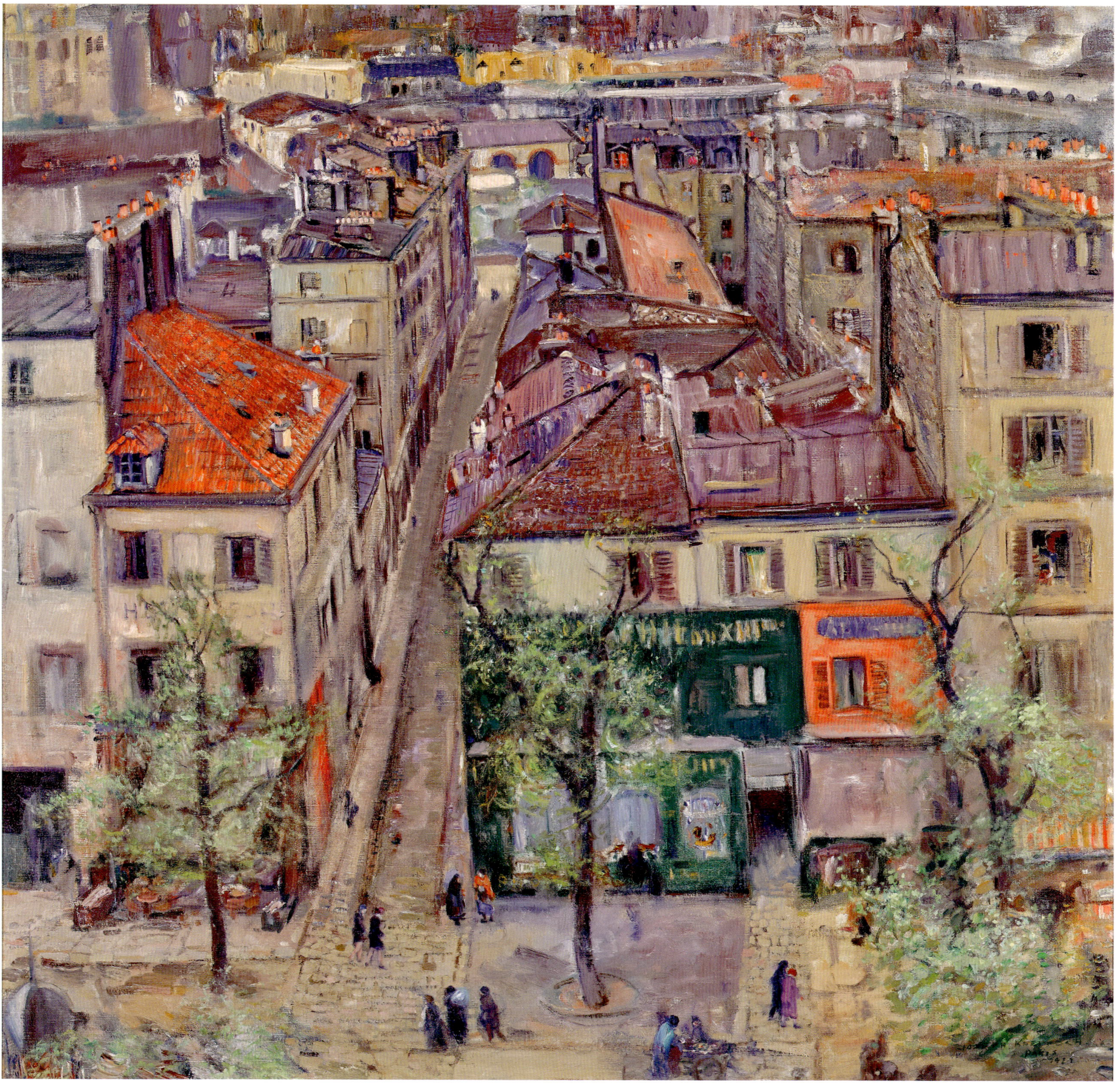

BLUE THREAD, 1927

Oil on canvas, 40 x 30 inches
Orange County Museum of Art Collection, Newport Beach, CA;
gift of Mr. and Mrs. Donald Winston

DURING HIS RESIDENCE IN EUROPE, Kleitsch made several spontaneous studies of colorful gardens in Paris, such as those at Luxembourg Gardens, the Tuileries, and the Place du Carrousel. However, he was still involved with figurative and portrait painting, as shown by this portrait of a single figure titled *Blue Thread*. Unlike his portraits of young, attractive Parisian ladies, here he has chosen for his subject an older, more matronly, French woman, bending over her sewing basket. Some Los Angeles critics were impressed with this vivid and realistic portrait and commented on the subject's "fine character, racial quality and the magnificent composition of full curving masses." Kleitsch had been studying some of the European masters' interior scenes of women sewing and embroidering, as painted by Diego Velázquez (1599–1660) and Jean-Baptiste-Siméon Chardin (1699–1779). Among Kleitsch's several paintings of this subject is a large half-length portrait (*Blue Thread*) modeled after a similar composition by Velázquez titled *The Needlewoman* (c. 1640–50).

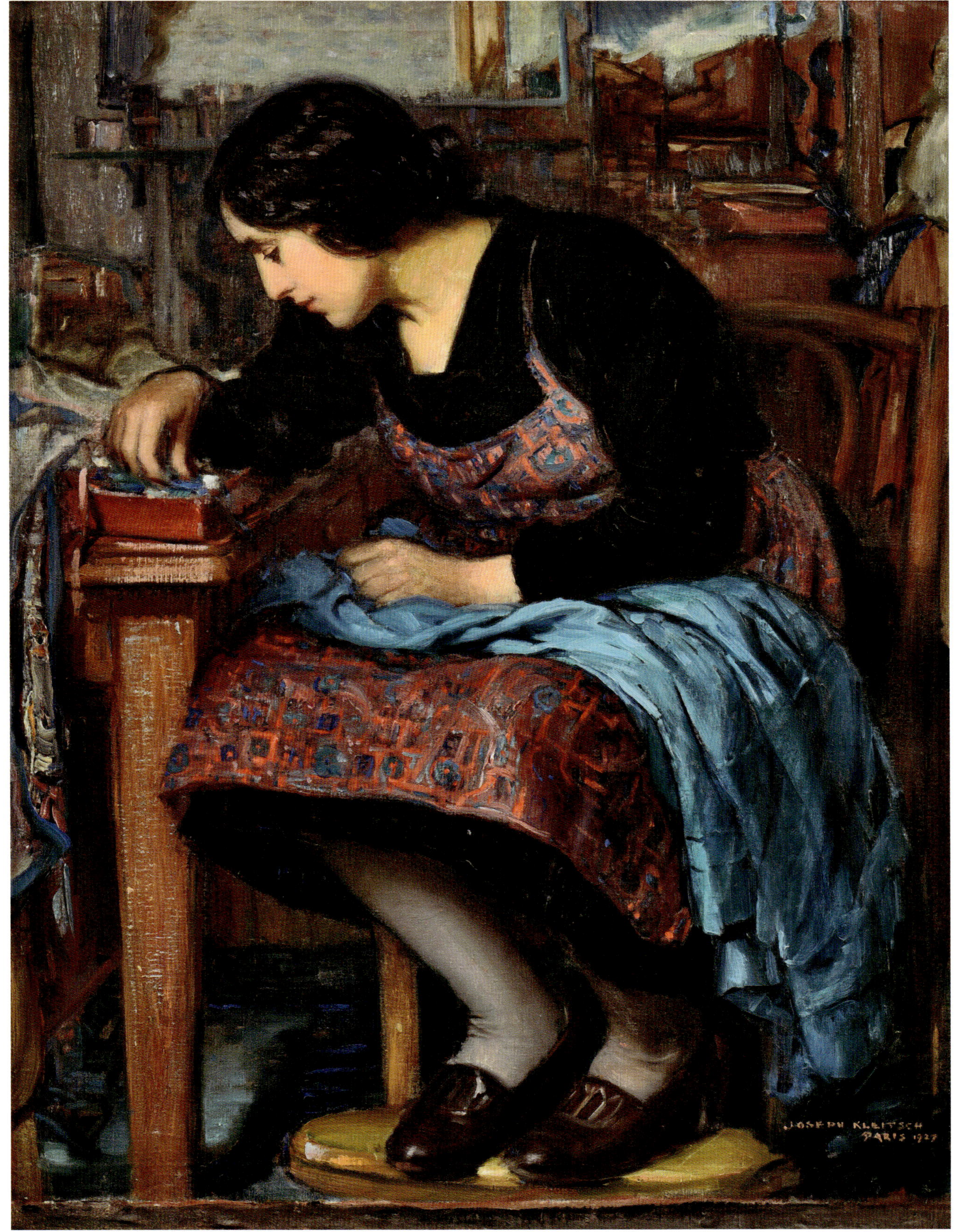
JOSEPH KLEITSCH
PARIS 1927

REFLECTIONS, VERNON (MLLE. AT TABLE), 1927

Oil on canvas, 34 x 34 inches
Private Collection

SEVERAL OTHER FIGURAL INTERIOR SCENES, including *Reflections,* seem to have been inspired by the paintings of such French masters as Manet, Monet, and Matisse. Kleitsch's European trip gave him the opportunity to visit museums and galleries to view the masters' art, which undoubtedly contributed to the growth of his own career. Here, like Manet's masterpiece *A Bar at the Folies-Bergère* (1882), Kleitsch has posed an attractive French woman in front of a mirror, at a Vernon hotel restaurant. The painting's visual complexity stems from the reflection in the mirror and the diffused light from the windows. Some commentators have posited that the sitter might be Edna, because of the strong resemblance between the two women, but she is actually an acquaintance or *amour* of the artist whose identity remains a mystery.

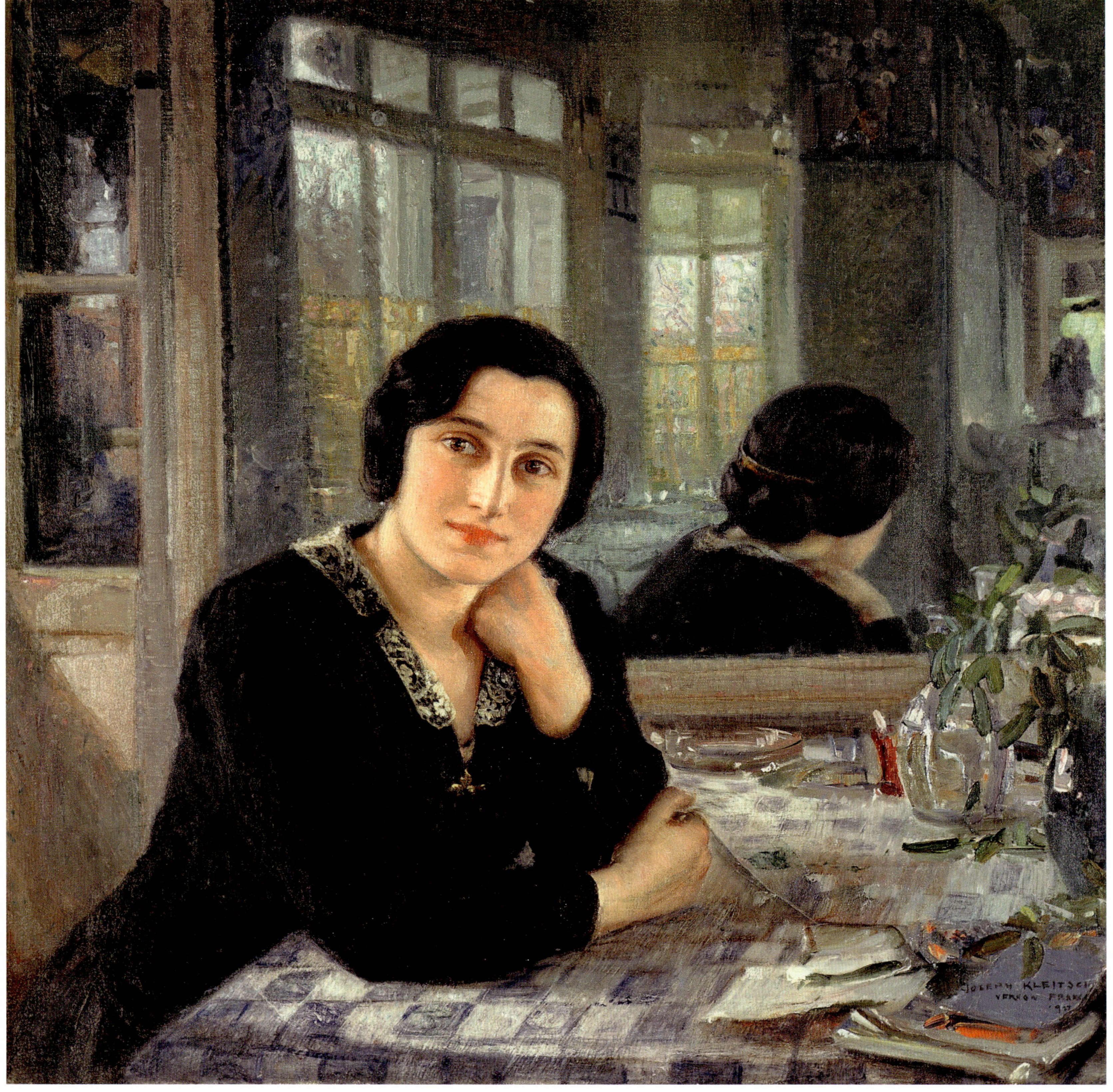
JOSEPH KLEITSCH
VERNON

REPOSER, PONT NEUF, PARIS, 1927

Oil on canvas, 36 x 36 inches
Collection of Reed and Christine Halladay

IN KLEITSCH'S EXPLORATION of Paris and its arrondissements, he was most attracted by the activity along the quays and below the many bridges of the Seine, in the heart of the Latin Quarter and on the Right Bank. Kleitsch chose to bring the viewer to the underside of Paris for the painting titled *Reposer*. The picture expresses the abject despair of hopeless derelicts through its somber tones. Kleitsch heightens the effect by placing himself, with his art paraphernalia, inside the composition; he serves as an observer of the depressing scene in order to give it a more realistic portrayal. The strong illumination through the arch in the bridge offers contrast and relief to this somber picture of desperation. Kleitsch's comical and perverse nature, as noted by his fellow members of the Palette and Chisel Club, is highlighted with the inclusion of a dog relieving itself on a trash container. For Kleitsch's work, this picture is rather unique in its evocation of deep human emotions.

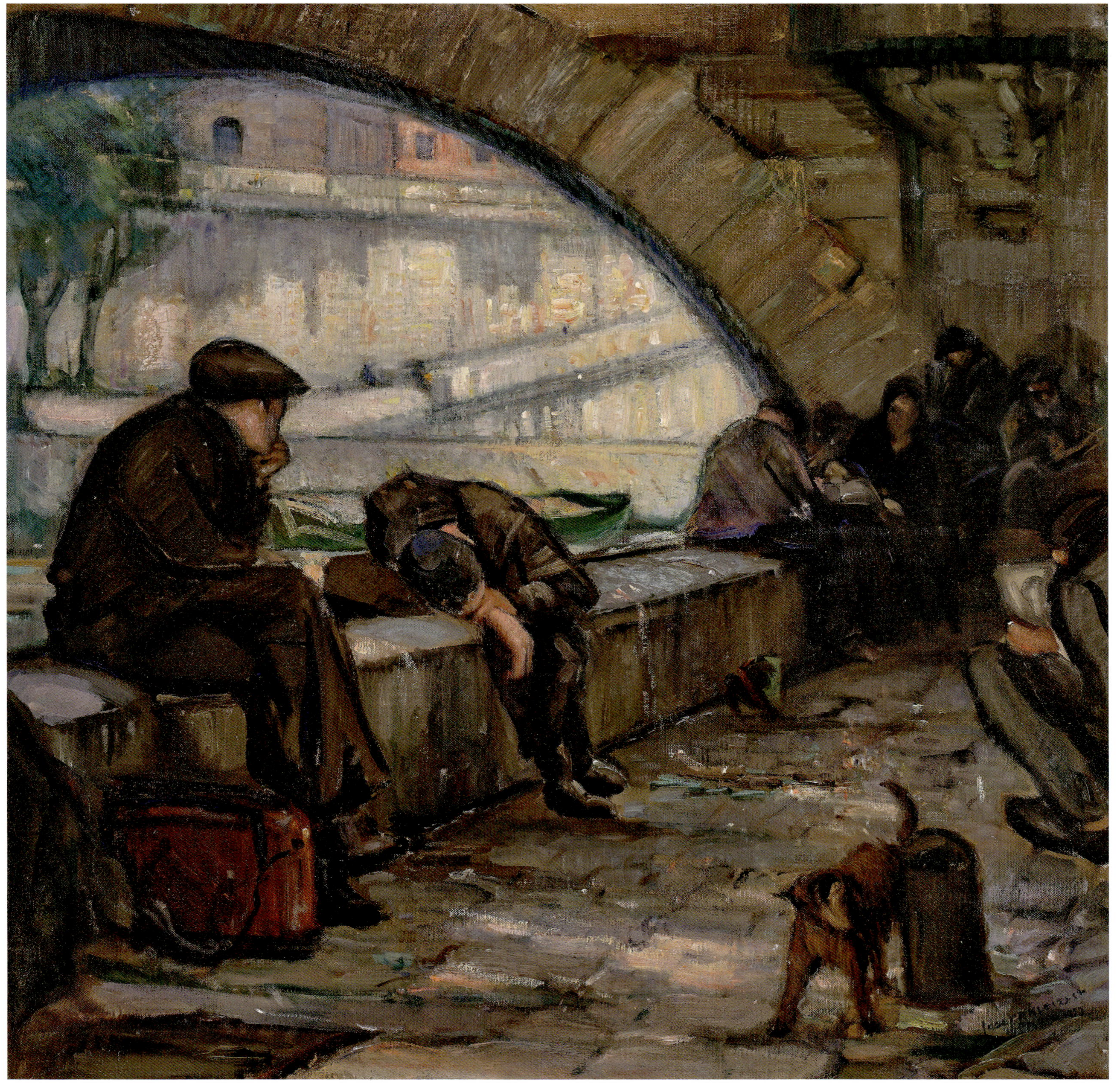

BATHERS ALONG THE SEINE, VERNON, FRANCE, 1926

Oil on canvas, 28 x 34 inches
Private Collection

DURING HIS FIRST VISIT to the Normandy village of Vernon, Kleitsch became enamored with a family of bathers, some in the nude, on the grassy banks of the Seine, enjoying the cool waters on a hot summer day after lunch. *Bathers* is a spontaneous study in vibrant color captured by Kleitsch, showing an everyday activity along the river. The short, broken brushstrokes and soft colors of the artist's palette indicate that he was moving toward a more impressionistic painting style. He was inspired by the artist Abel Warshawsky (1883–1962), who accompanied Kleitsch on his 1926 trip to Vernon, along with two of Warshawsky's friends. The provocative nude bathers, others partially clothed, are summarily treated, foretelling Kleitsch's treatment of figures in his later Laguna Beach scenes.

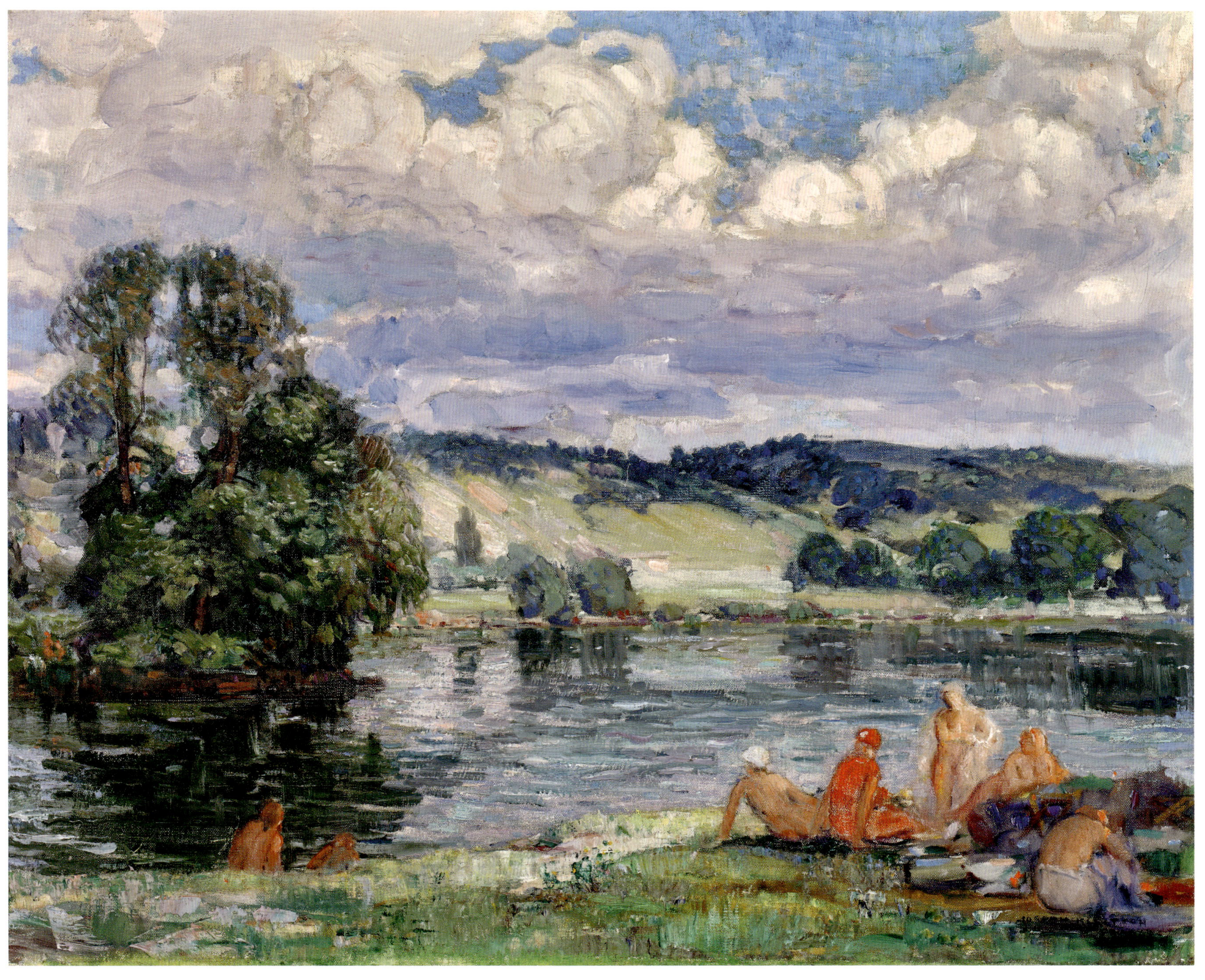

SELF-PORTRAIT, 1909

Oil on canvas, 54 x 38 inches
Private Collection

THE ACCESSIBILITY OF Old Master paintings in museums worldwide enabled the budding artist to study closely the renowned works of Dürer, Rembrandt, Frans Hals, and others. Albrecht Dürer (1471–1528), a Northern Renaissance master, is considered the progenitor of the independent self-portrait. Some one hundred years later, as one art historian has written, "Rembrandt scrutinized himself before the mirror, painting, etching, and drawing his changing physique and physiognomy as well as the varying psychological states that reflected the fluctuating fortunes of his life" (Steven Platzman, *Cézanne: The Self-Portraits*, 2001). Indeed, artists have been gazing into mirrors to depict the outer and inner image of themselves since the late Middle Ages. Cézanne (1839–1906) painted himself with unusual candor while looking into the mirror as he worked.

While the style and iconography of a self-portrait may portray the outer artist's historical persona, it is the underlying configuration of the portrait that reveals the inner self. It has been argued that a self-portrait marks a point of personal transition amid changes and events in an artist's life. The artist finds his own body a convenient subject of observation, eliminating the need for a model, but this could be a false interpretation of one's self-image much refracted by the experience of life. Then the question is asked: "Is it a meaningful portal to the artist's persona?"

Kleitsch's progression in his artistic career is chronicled by four self-portraits, painted at various stages of his colorful and dynamic life. Created at important junctures in his career and life, these provide an opportunity to understand the artist's persona. They also suggest the artist's inner self, leading to a psychological analysis of the painter during these transitions.

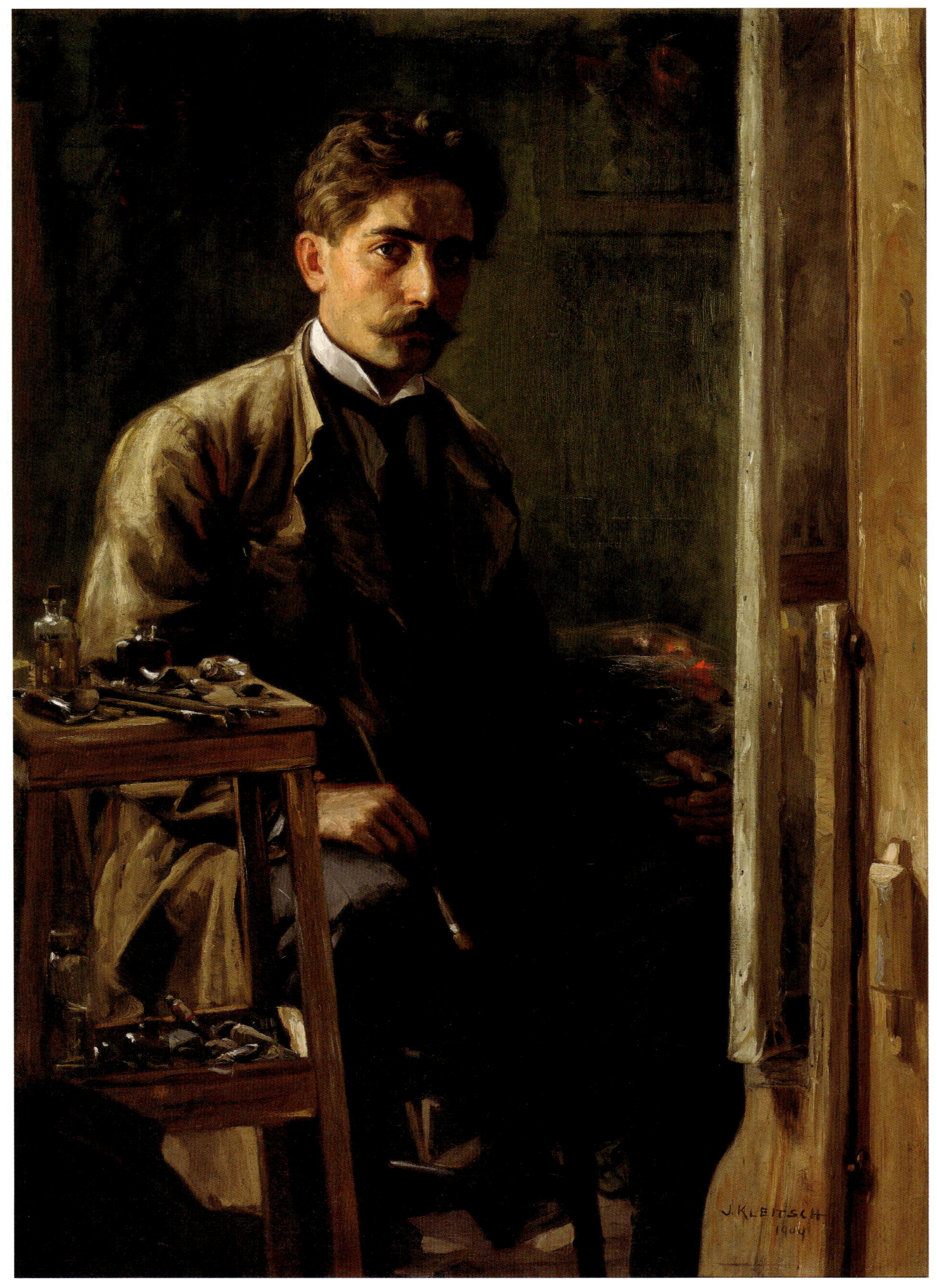
J. KLEITSCH

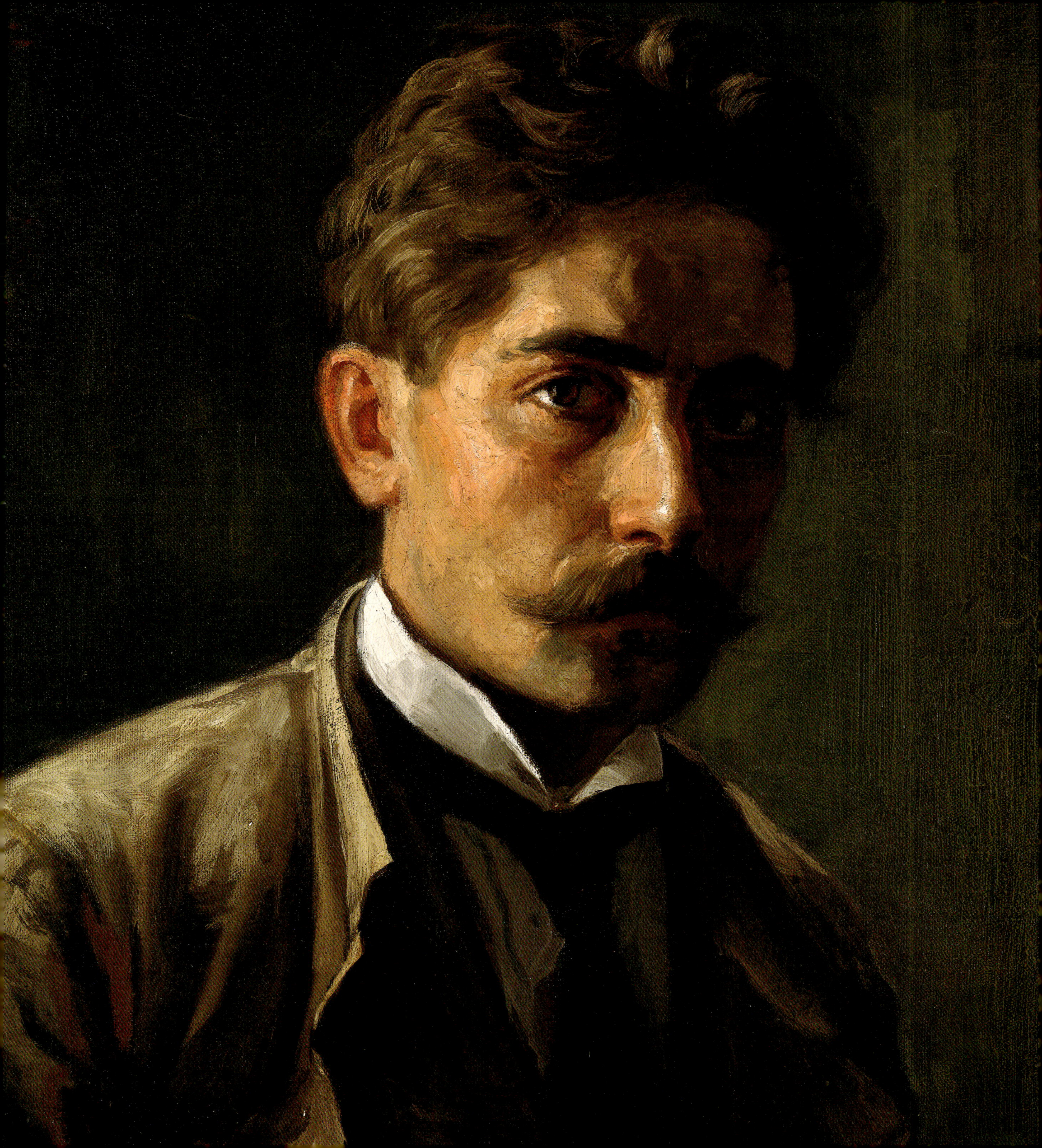

In 1909, at twenty-seven years of age and living in Mexico City with his wife Emma, Kleitsch painted a seated, three-quarter-length self-portrait that recalls the dark-colored tonal brushwork of the Munich School. While living in Denver, Kleitsch had become close friends with William C. Baker, an Easterner formerly employed by the Union Pacific Railroad. When they both experienced financial difficulties, the loquacious Baker persuaded Kleitsch and his wife, twenty-five years his senior, to establish low-cost residency in Mexico City. There, Baker, an accomplished photographer, snapped a photo of Kleitsch seated at his easel, with his wife beside him. Kleitsch's financial condition and the modesty of his furnished lodgings are apparent, as is a large hole in the sole of his shoe. Despite his hard luck, the artist expanded his repertoire and executed several paintings and drawings in the academic-realist style.

His 1909 self-portrait, painted in Mexico, is less tentative than his earlier portrait paintings from Denver (though no record exists of any professional art training in Mexico). In this portrait, he captures his youthful appearance but, in spite of his hesitant self-assurance, projects an image of a successful professional. This points to the future, when appearance will become more important to him, and his apparel will represent an awareness of changing fashions. In this self-portrait, his appearance is fastidious, evident by the neatly knotted tie, the artist's smock worn over his business suit, the well-trimmed moustache, and the hair tousled but within fashionable bounds. In keeping with the new mode of dress in the first decade of the twentieth century, he wears a carefully tailored business suit and a white, wing-collared shirt with a dark, patterned tie. With the intensity of his furrowed brow and his piercing eyes, Kleitsch attempts to present a more mature image of himself.

Kleitsch's 1909 self-portrait shows "a deep, youthful self-involvement, bordering on narcissistic self-absorption," as one writer speculated about a Cézanne self-portrait that he felt had made the artist look upon himself to find "the emerging creative force" (Platzman, ibid.) Kleitsch's youthful self-portrait, like those of Rembrandt and others, led to the admission of vulnerability evident in his later confrontations with his persona. The self-portraits he executed over his career challenge both formal concerns and psychological interpretations and mark definite transitions in his life and career.

SELF-PORTRAIT, 1915

Oil on canvas, 40 x 30 inches
Collection of James Taylor and Gary Conway

IN 1915, AT THIRTY-THREE YEARS OF AGE, Kleitsch was awarded a prestigious medal for two portraits exhibited in the Palette and Chisel Club annual, an award given "for the most creditable work by a member." He and Edgar Payne were cited among the club's exhibitors as "the strong painters of several seasons" (*Chicago Herald Examiner,* April 22, 1915). As Kleitsch's paintings gained acceptance, his self-assurance grew, his work broadened, and its quality improved. In the same banner year, his self-portrait of 1915 was exhibited in the Art Institute's Nineteenth Annual Exhibition by Artists of Chicago and Vicinity, and his demeanor in it reflects a career that is flourishing. With the new responsibilities of a recent marriage and a child on the way, his appearance suggests a man who is beginning to mature and improve his station in life. His recent recognition by the art community of Chicago is suggested by his posture and dress—the fedora set at a jaunty angle, the colorful, futurist-patterned cravat, and the red pin on his coat lapel (possibly the French Légion d'honneur?)—reflect a confident Kleitsch. The large overcoat with wide lapels, business suit, vest, and gloves complete this image of the artist as a mainline success with an ever-expanding career. The eyes are interesting because they, too, reflect a confidence not evident in his 1909 self-portrait (p. 127). For fashion-conscious expatriate American James Abbott McNeill Whistler (1834–1903), "dress [also] played an essential role in his portraits . . . as an indicator of the character and status of the sitter" (Susan Grace Galassi, "Whistler, Women, and Fashion," *American Art Review* 15 [2003]: 96). This self-affirming portrait marks another significant transition in Kleitsch's life and career.

Kleitsch would paint a much more sober self-portrait in 1917, just after America entered the First World War. He had only lived in the country for a decade and a half, and he no doubt felt the horrors of war particularly acutely; there is even evidence that he tried to hide his German ancestry.

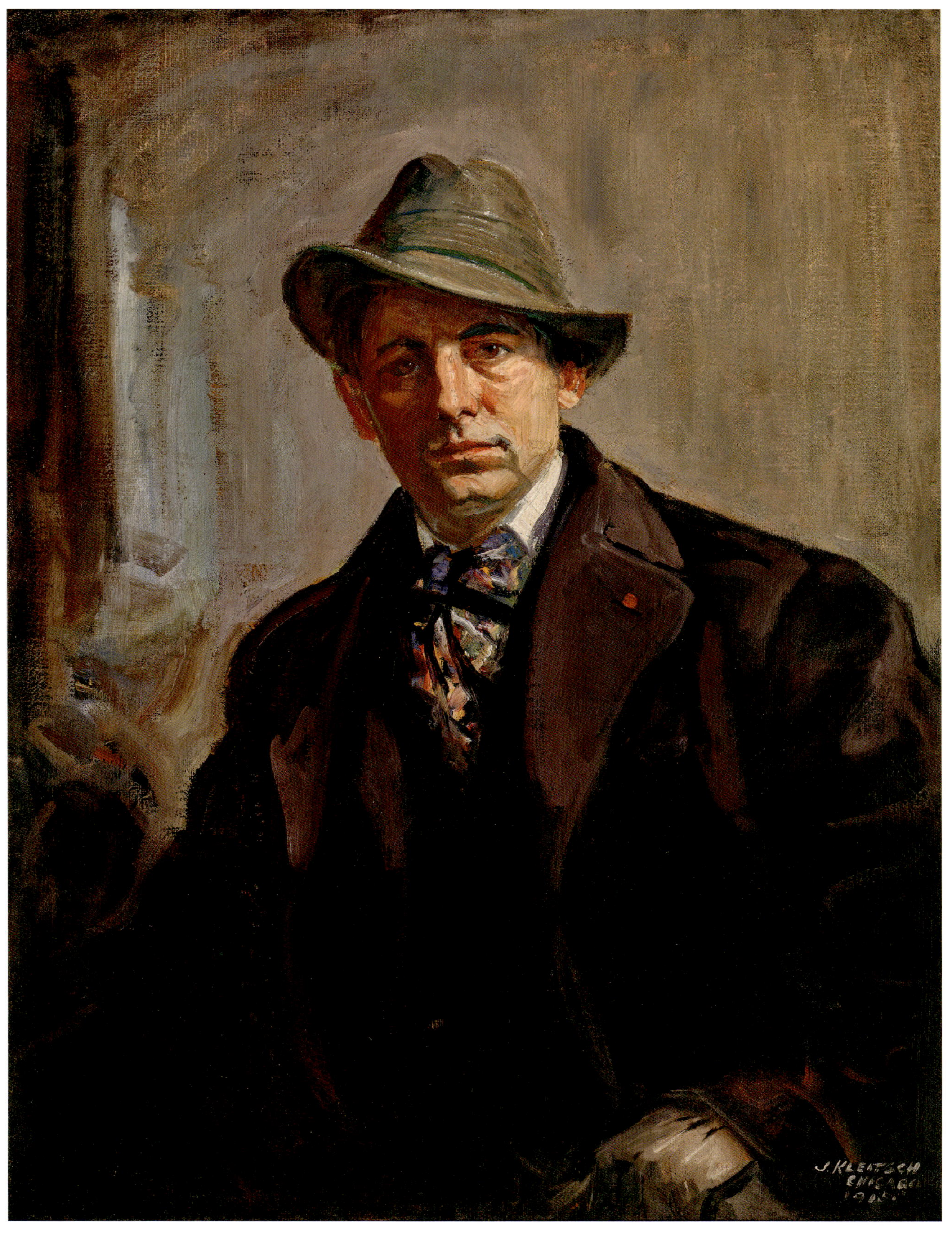
J. KLEITSCH
CHICAGO

SELF-PORTRAIT, 1919

Oil on canvas, 30 x 24 inches
Collection of Mary Olden

THE ARTIST REACHED THE PINNACLE of his career in Chicago when his self-portrait of 1919 was accepted in the Art Institute's Thirty-Second Annual Exhibition of American Oil Paintings and Sculpture, held in December of that year. It was a clear indication that the painters from the East Coast no longer enjoyed exclusivity in the event, as the annuals were now open to the cadre of Western artists.

At this point in his career, Kleitsch planned to make a trip abroad in order to broaden his artistic experience; however, rumors in local newspapers suggested that he and Edna had disagreed about his plans, and that they had settled their differences by moving to California. Kleitsch's self-portrait of 1919 reflects the serious side of his nature and his resolution to further advance his art career in a new environment. The intensity of his eyes suggests a passionate desire to build upon his newfound success. The almost frontal pose, showing him surrounded by the tools of his trade, seems specifically autobiographical, hinting at a certain vulnerability but also marking a significant transition in his artistic lifestyle.

Because Kleitsch's 1909 self-portrait (p. 127) was based on William Baker's photographs, he is shown painting with his right hand, but here in this 1919 portrait he used a mirror, reversing the image. The artist paints with his left hand and supports the palette with his right. While in Paris in 1926, he painted a casual, almost full-length self-portrait also using a mirror. Because this portrait is a mirror image, the artist's right hand is in his pocket as he paints with his left. From the evidence here, Kleitsch was right handed.

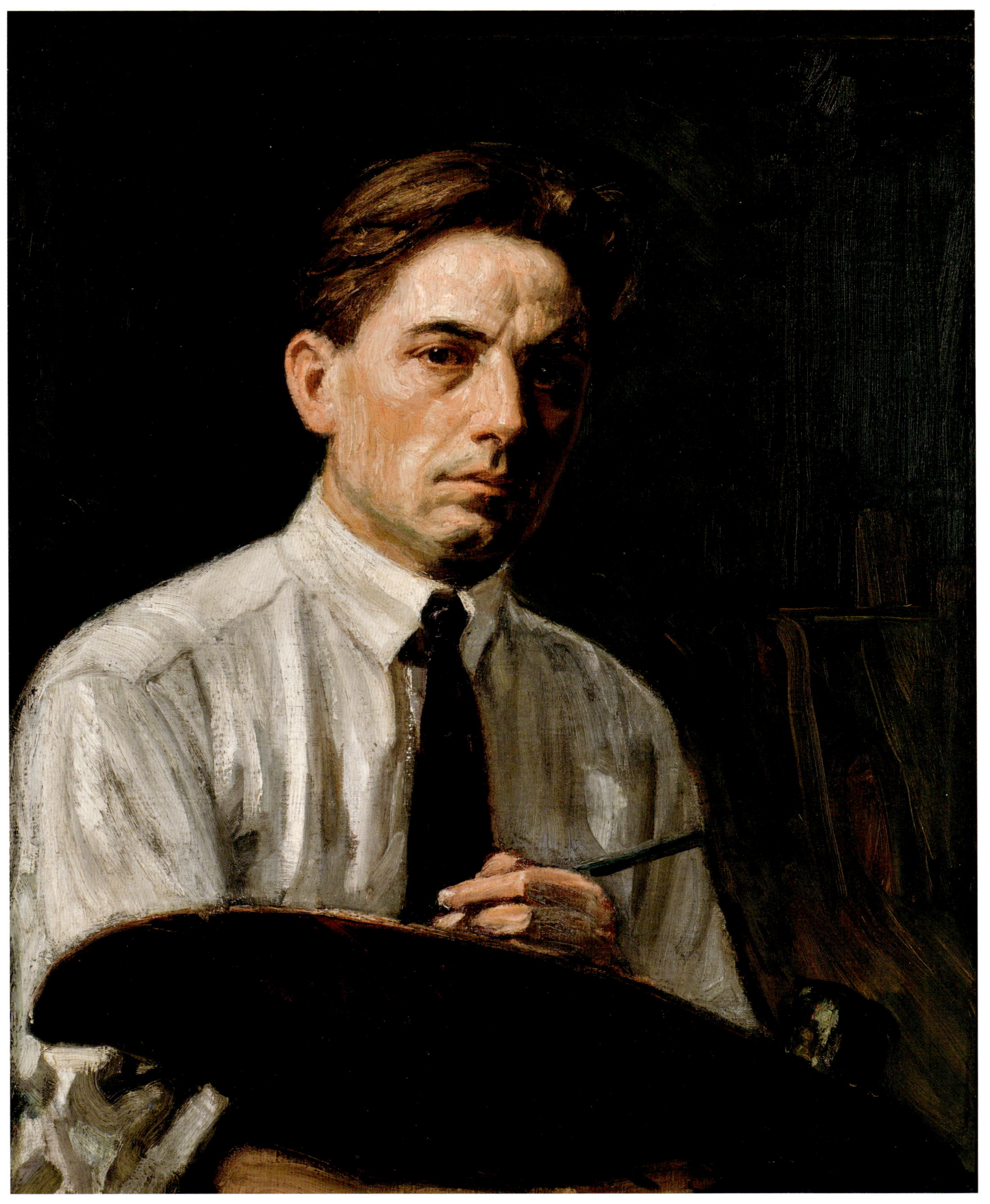

SELF-PORTRAIT (GRAND RAPIDS, MICHIGAN), 1925

Oil on canvas, 30 x 22 inches
Orange County Museum of Art Collection, Newport Beach, CA;
gift of Mr. and Mrs. Roy Childs

ON A CROSS-COUNTRY TRIP in 1925, just before Kleitsch left for an extended trip to Europe, he and his family stopped in Chicago and were feted by friends, colleagues, and collectors. Their next stop was Grand Rapids, where Edna had lived as a child; they visited her parents, who still resided and worked there. The Kleitsch family stayed at the Rowe Hotel, the social center of Grand Rapids, projecting an image of the artist's successful career to the local population.

During their brief stay, the artist painted a unique self-portrait in a landscape setting. Kleitsch's demeanor, with furrowed brow and confrontational eyes looking at the viewer, project a very serious side or mood of the artist's persona, unlike his previous self-portraits. The impending dynamic change in the course of his career, without the support of his colleagues and friends, may have been unsettling, as he reflected on what sort of reception he would receive in Europe. With his palette in hand, standing on a hill overlooking the river, the artist is the picture of maturity and self-confidence. His well-trimmed Vandyke beard enhances his image as a successful practitioner of the arts. While working outdoors, he wears a shirt with a cutaway collar and a hand-painted tie tucked under a vest, part of a three-piece suit. A felt hat completes the de rigueur ensemble. The season can be verified by the autumnal colors and cornstalks in the background. In the far distance across the river, the smokestacks of many furniture factories are visible, indicating that the portrait was painted in a rural setting near a large industrial city.

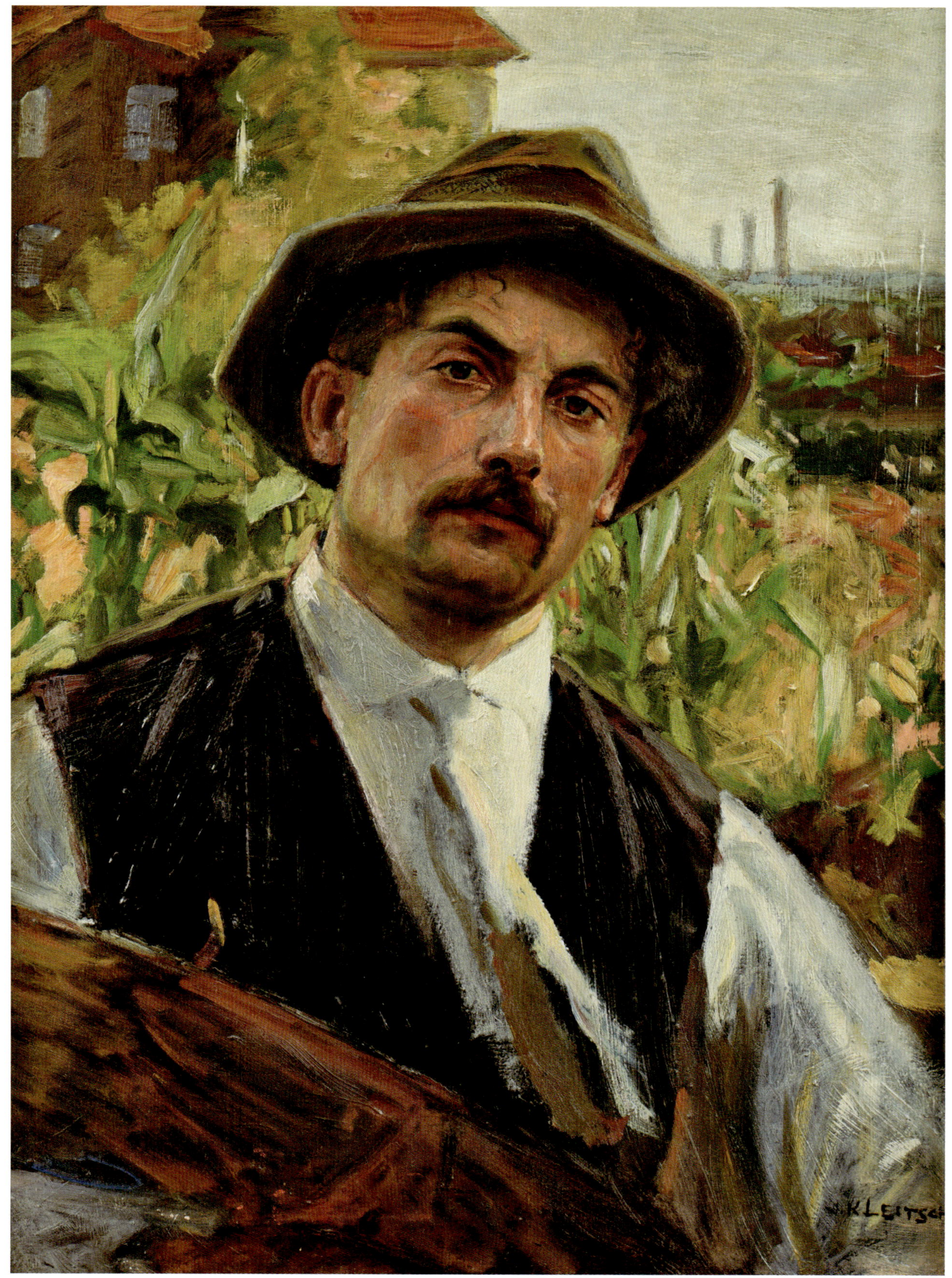
J. KLEITSCH

EXHIBITION CHECKLIST

Studio Portraits & Genre Scenes

The Artist's Wife, 1919
Oil on canvas
62 ¼ x 52 inches
Collection of Simon K. Chiu
p. 47

Miss Ketchum, c. 1918
Oil on canvas
42 x 36 inches
Private Collection
p. 51

The Attic Philosopher, 1916
Oil on canvas
36 x 28 inches
Collection of Mr. and Mrs. Thomas B. Stiles II
p. 53

Problematicus, 1918
Oil on canvas
60 x 55 inches
Collection of Robert and Susan Ehrlich
p. 55

Portrait of Isador Berger (Rhapsody), 1917
Oil on canvas
40 x 30 inches
Private Collection
p. 57

Miss Gregg, c. 1919
Oil on canvas
48 x 30 inches
Collection of Michael Kizhner Fine Art
p. 59

Portrait of Dr. Walter Jarvis Barlow. c. 1921–22
Oil on canvas
36 x 32 inches
Collection of Barlow Respiratory Hospital
p. 61

Portrait of Robert Fullonton, 1921
Oil on canvas
40 x 34 inches
Laguna Art Museum Collection, Gift of Marjory Adams Darling
p. 63

The Oriental Shop, 1922
Oil on canvas
32 x 40 inches
Crocker Art Museum, Melza and Ted Barr Collection
p. 65

The Oriental Shop (The Jade Shop), 1925
Oil on canvas
32 x 26 inches
The Irvine Museum
p. 67

William Kleitsch, c. 1910–15
Oil on canvas
40 x 30 inches
Private Collection
p. 69

Behind the Fence, c. 1910–11
Oil on canvas
38 x 24 inches
Courtesy of The Redfern Gallery
p. 71

Studio Interior, 1915
Oil on canvas
30 x 40 inches
Collection of Simon K. Chiu
p. 73

Untitled Portrait in Athenaeum Club Room, c. 1915
Oil on canvas
33 x 25 inches
Collection of James Taylor and Gary Conway
p. 75

Untitled, 1911
Oil on canvas
46 x 34 inches
Private Collection, from the Estate of Pearl Martin
p. 77

Portrait of Ruth Renick (Jade Necklace), 1928
Oil on canvas
35 ½ x 39 inches
Collection of Larane Rodnick
p. 79

Portrait of Mildred Lawrence, 1922
Oil on canvas
24 x 22 ½ inches
Courtesy of George Stern Fine Arts
p. 81

Laguna, New & Old

Café las Ondas, c. 1930
Oil on canvas
32 x 39 ½ inches
Private Collection, from the Estate of Pearl Martin
p. 83

Laguna Avenue and Hotel Laguna, 1930
Oil on canvas
36 x 40 inches
Collection of William Selman
p. 85

Laguna on a Cloudy Day (Main Beach), c. 1930
Oil on canvas
36 x 40 inches
Private Collection, from the Estate of Pearl Martin
p. 87

Nudes, c. 1929–30
Oil on canvas
20 ½ x 18 inches
Collection of Linda and David O'Hoy
p. 89

Ocean Front—Main Beach, Laguna, c. 1929–30
Oil on canvas
36 x 40 inches
Collection of Stephen P. Diamond, M.D.
p. 91

Laguna Road II, c. 1929–30
Oil on canvas
36 x 40 inches
Private Collection
p. 93

El Paseo, 1928–29
Oil on canvas
30 x 40 inches
Private Collection
p. 95

Enchantment, 1922
Oil on canvas
22 x 18 ¼ inches
Private Collection
p. 97

Under the Eucalyptus Trees, 1922
Oil on canvas
45 x 35 inches
Private Collection
p. 99

Comrades, c. 1928
Oil on canvas
40 x 36 inches
Collection of Ken Mizushima
p. 101

Beachcombers, c. 1928
Oil on canvas
26 x 30 inches
Courtesy of The Kelley Gallery and George Stern Fine Arts
p. 103

Mission San Juan Capistrano

Red and Green (Mission San Juan Capistrano), 1923
Oil on canvas
36 x 40 inches
The Irvine Museum
p. 107

El Peón [José Juan Olivares] or *Old Man Yorba, San Juan Capistrano*, 1923
Oil on canvas
30 x 25 inches
Collection of James W. and Sarah T. Miller
p. 109

The Story Teller (Eugene and El Peón [José Juan Olivares]), 1925
Oil on canvas
18 x 22 inches
Collection of William Selman
p. 111

Curiosity (Mission San Juan Capistrano), 1924
Oil on canvas
25 x 30 inches
Collection Mr. and Mrs. Thomas B. Stiles II
p. 113

Going to Church (Sunday Morning), Capistrano, 1924
Oil on canvas
40 x 36 inches
Private Collection
p. 115

Sojourn in Europe

Paris, 1926
Oil on canvas
36 x 36 inches
Collection of W. Donald Head, Old Grandview Ranch
p. 117

Blue Thread, 1927
Oil on canvas
40 x 30 inches
Orange County Museum of Art Collection, Newport Beach, CA; gift of Mr. and Mrs. Donald Winston
p. 119

Reflections, Vernon (Mlle. at Table), 1927
Oil on canvas
34 x 34 inches
Private Collection
p. 121

Reposer, Pont Neuf, Paris, 1927
Oil on canvas
36 x 36 inches
Collection of Reed and Christine Halladay
p. 123

Bathers along the Seine, Vernon, France, 1926
Oil on canvas
28 x 34 inches
Private Collection
p. 125

Self-Portraits

Self-Portrait, 1909
Oil on canvas
54 x 38 inches
Private Collection
p. 127

Self-Portrait, 1915
Oil on canvas
40 x 30 inches
Collection of James Taylor and Gary Conway
p. 131

Self-Portrait, 1919
Oil on canvas
30 x 24 inches
Collection of Mary Olden
p. 133

Self-Portrait (Grand Rapids, Michigan), 1925
Oil on canvas
30 x 22 inches
Orange County Museum of Art Collection, Newport Beach, CA; gift of Mr. and Mrs. Roy Childs
p. 135

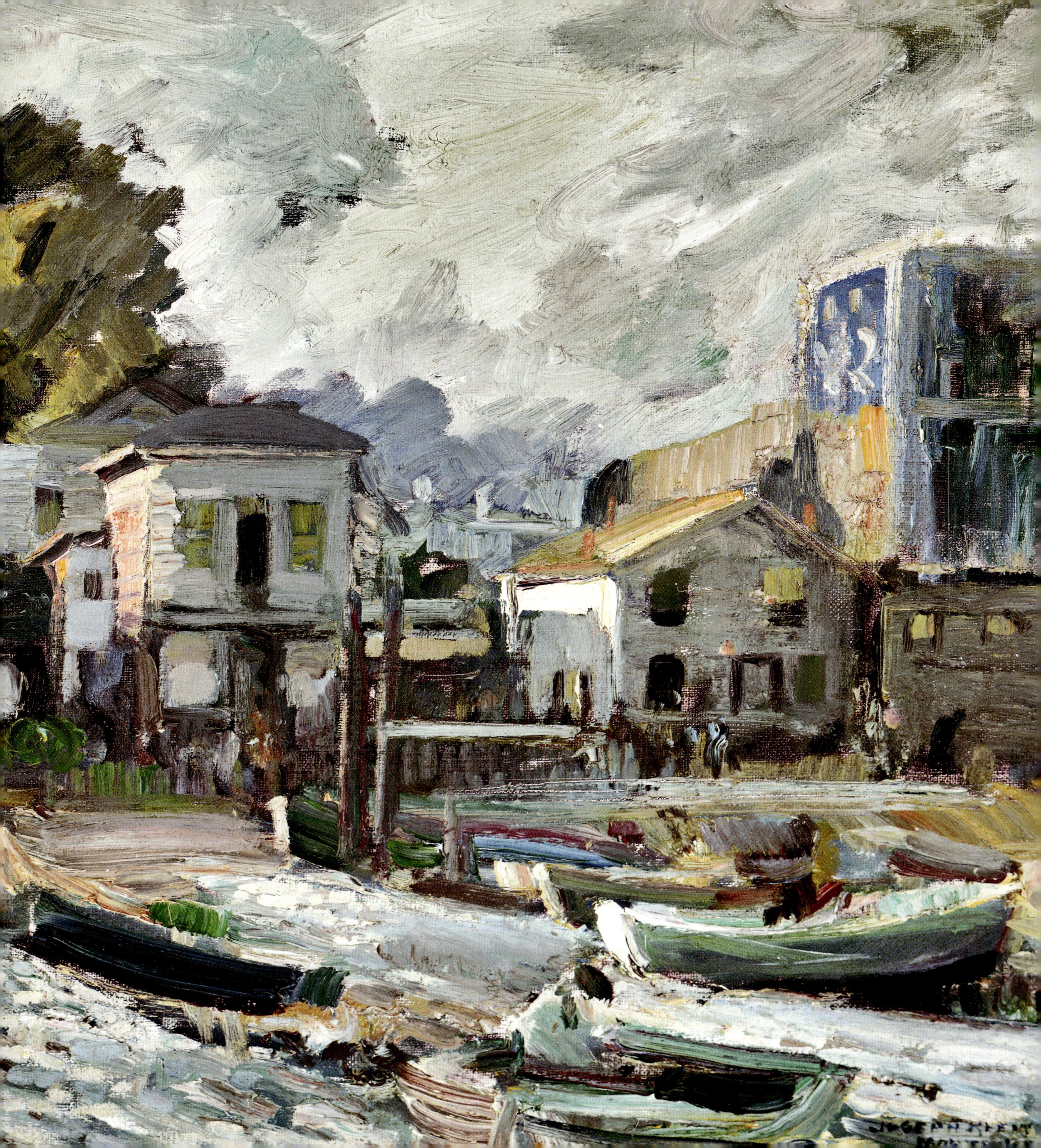

CONTRIBUTORS

The realization of *The Golden Twenties: Portraits and Figure Paintings by Joseph Kleitsch* and the accompanying catalogue has been made possible through the financial support of the following individuals and institutions.

Diane Asselin Baer
Bonhams Auctioneers
Yvonne Boseker
Simon K. Chiu
Susan and Jim Crawford
Bram and Sandra Dijkstra
Jeff Dutra
Susan and Robert Ehrlich
Michael Feddersen
Jerrold and Judith Felsenthal
Lauren Frankel
William C. Georges
Robert and Nadine Hall
Christine and Reed Halladay
The Historical Collections Council of California Art
Lori and Jeff Hyland
John Moran Auctioneers
Gina Knox
Hannah and Russel Kully
Allen and Dottie Lay
Joyce and Tom Leddy
Penny and Jay Lusche
Janet G. Michaels
Tobey Moss and Allen Moss
Gail and Peter Ochs
Bob and Arlene Oltman
The Redfern Gallery
Gayle and Ed Roski
Ann and Dan Selmi
Mel and Betty Sembler
Earlene and Herbert Seymour
Randy and Mary Short
Jonas B. Siegel
Diane and Van Simmons
Kathleen Lombard Smyk
Irene and George Stern
Lawrence H. Title
Carol and Cliff Trenton
Betsey Tyler
Ruth Westphal
Reba White Williams
Brooke Abercrombie and Christopher Wilson

Fish Market—Monterey (detail), 1923–24
Oil on canvas, 18 x 20 inches
Collection of Paul and Kathleen Bagley

Overleaf:
Curiosity (*Mission San Juan Capistrano*) (detail), 1924
Oil on canvas, 25 x 30 inches
Collection Mr. and Mrs. Thomas B. Stiles II

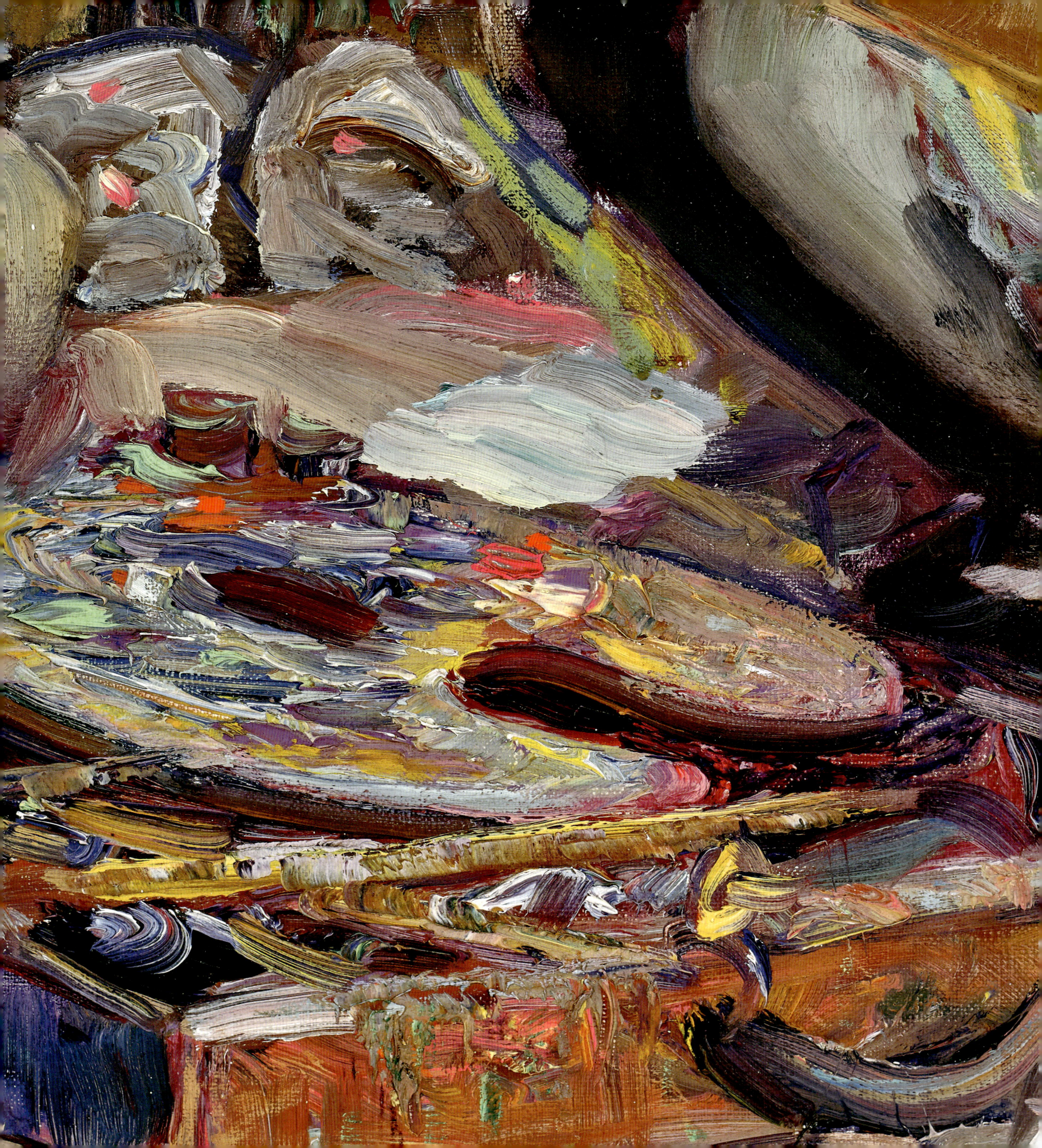